Seven Psychic Secrets

SEVEN PSYCHIC SECRETS

A Practical Guide To Developing Your Own Psychic Abilities

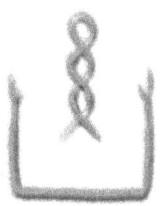

by Dr. Shé D'Montford

Seven Psychic Secrets

ISBN: 978-1-4710-2584-6
3rd Edition
24th February 2013
© Shé D'Montford
Happy Medium Publishing
P.O. Box 3541
Helensvale Town Centre Qld.
Gold Coast
Australia
For World Wide Distribution

THE HAPPY MEDIUM PUBLISHING COMPANY
THE MESSAGE IS IN THE MEDIUM

THE HAPPY MEDIUM PUBLISHING COMPANY
THE MESSAGE IS IN THE MEDIUM
Brings you: -

Seven Psychic Secrets

ISBN: 978-1-4710-2584-6

Shé D'Montford's "Seven Psychic Secrets" written by, cover design and layout Rev. Dr. S. D'Montford. Cover artwork by Wanda Shipton, created especially for this book. © Copyright Rev, Dr, S. D'Montford, Jan 1st 1996, this version revised Sunday, Feb 24th 2013 Gold Coast Australia. Published by THE HAPPY MEDIUM PUBLISHING COMPANY for educational purposes. ALL RIGHTS RESERVED. The information presented is protected under the Berne Convention for the Protection of Literature and Artistic works, under other international conventions and under national laws on copyright and neighbouring rights. Extracts of the information in this book may be reviewed, but not reproduced or translated without express written permission from the publisher. Reproduction or translation of portions of this publication requires explicit, prior authorization in writing. **Disclaimer:** The primary reason for this publication is entertainment and education about Pagan practices. While The Happy Medium Publishing Company and Shambhallah Awareness Centre has used all reasonable endeavours to ensure the information in this book is as accurate as possible, it gives no warranty or guarantee that the material, information, or publications made available by them are fit for any use whatsoever and require that you use your own commonsense in working with any materials provided THE HAPPY MEDIUM PUBLISHING COMPANY, Shambhallah Awareness Centre and Rev. Dr S. D'Montford accepts no liability or responsibility for any loss or damage whatsoever suffered as a result of direct or indirect use or application of any material, publication or information obtained from them. THE HAPPY MEDIUM PUBLISHING COMPANY is a division of Shambhallah Awareness Centre a tax exempt Pagan Church and a not for profit organization. P.O. Box 3541, Helensvale Town Centre. Q. 4212 http://www.shambhallah.org Special Thanks to:- Wanda Shipton, Ken Wills, Dylan Lawrence, Lucas Preedy, Kushog and all the persons who have participated in my classes for the last 30-years.

Contents: -

1. **Why It Works**
On page 7

2. **How It Works**
On page 37

Skill 1

3. **Seeing Auras**
On page 59

Skill 2

4. **Feeling & Moving Energy**
On page 79

Skill 3

5. **Working With Spirit**
On page 107

Skill 4

6. **Psychometry**
On page 131

Skill 5

7. **Remote Viewing**
On page 141

Skill 6

8. **Medical Intuition**
On page 149

Skill 7

9. **Healing & Remote Healing**
On page 159

10. **The Journey Begins**
On page 175

Shé D'Montford's
SEVEN PSYCHIC SECRETS

A Practical Guide To Developing Your Own Psychic Abilities

> *You saw her on the Channel 7 smash hit psychic T.V. show "The One." After displaying her astounding abilities and their practical applications, Viewers voted Shé as the most gifted and compassionate.*
>
> *Here Shé shares her psychic secrets with you, in a clear concise and down-to-earth way so that you too can be 'The One.'*
>
> *Throw away all the other 'How to be a psychic' manuals.*
>
> *This is the only One you will ever need!*

Upon this day and from this hour
You can stand in your full power

It is your birthright to be all that you can be.

When you develop your own psychic abilities, you begin living in a much larger world.

These abilities are completely natural.

Adding the spiritual realms to this mundane existence brings depth and richness to life.

Being trained in these abilities gives you the edge.
You become empowered.

Once you have gained metaphysical mastery you can begin to truly help other people.

Life can be a magical experience.

Let me show you how...

Seven Psychic Secrets

Why It Works

Why? It Works!

If you know how and why this stuff works and you are keen to get stuck straight into the psychic development techniques, then skip this chapter.

The constant badgering and bulling of psychics over these questions demands a reply beyond, **"No one really knows why and how, it just does!"** This chapter is for those that sincerely want to examine these questions, in simple terms, without psychobabble.

A Word To The Skeptics

"All truths are easy to understand once they are discovered; the point is to discover them."

said Galileo Galilei the Italian natural philosopher, astronomer and mathematician who made fundamental contributions to the development of the scientific method and to the sciences of motion, astronomy and strength of materials. The skeptics of his day kept him under house arrest until his death in 1642 for his assertions that the earth was round and not the centre of the universe.

At about the same time, through out Europe, those who practiced traditional medicine, the midwives and herbalists, were being slaughtered by those skeptical that something unseen could be responsible for disease. Hygiene was seen as a superstitious Pagan practice, a legacy of the heathen schools of Pythagoras in the "modern" age. The result of that wave of fanatical skepticism was The Black Plague, costing over eight million lives. [1]

Ironically, it was Nostradamus' success in treating people with this disease and his renown in preventing its spread that was instrumental in returning the practice of hygiene to the burgeoning medical profession. Yet, if it were not for the protection of the King of France, the skeptics of his day would have had him killed for it too!

Though skeptics have had many a dark hour, and have been responsible for many atrocities, we need skeptics. Thank you to all the skeptics for being there. It generally helps us. Most psychics are skeptics that have been exposed to something that mainstream science struggles to explain. Once exposed, these people begin researching and experimenting with explanations for their unusual experiences.

Real psychics do not make any absolute "truth" claims about these phenomena; they are still seeking to understand the experiences that are happening to them.

> *"It is a capital mistake to theorize before one has data."*
> Sherlock Holmes/Arthur Conan Doyle

Psychics do not need anybody to believe them; they just do what they do and keep trying to gather data and experiences.

Many psychics suspend judgment in their investigations and therefore, by definition, they are 'Pyrrhonists' or true philosophical skeptics. Nevertheless, they are not 'Sophists' who, as Socrates said, "are those who seek to reason away all things." Sophist is the correct term for pseudo-skepticism, which makes negative claims without bearing the burden of proof of those claims. There is no point in taking the opposing argument just for arguments sake. It is a waste of effort and proves nothing either way.

Real skeptics hate pseudo-skeptics the same way that real psychics hate fraudulent ones. Frauds give the real thing a bad reputation. Psychics love debunking frauds. Genuine psychics and genuine skeptics can work very well together to accomplish this. In fact, they did for six years as shown by Harry Houdini, the famous stage magician.

Harry Houdini - A Paranormal Believer and Skeptic
The first skeptic society was formed in the 1920s after Harry Houdini wrote two books "Miracle Mongers and Their Methods" in 1920 and "A Magician Among the Spirits" in 1924, about his methods for exposing the tricks of fraudulent mediums. In fact, the stage name "Houdini" was borrowed from Jean Eugene Robert "Houdini" a famous French illusionist from the late 1800s, who became well known for exposing those who perform fake religious miracles.

Harry Houdini embarked upon his debunking exploits with Sir Arthur Conan Doyle, the famous author of the Sherlock Holmes novels who was a driving force in the fledgling Spiritualist groups. Sherlock Holms was Gene Rodenberry's inspiration for the logical Star Trek science officer Mr. Spock. Many of Conan-Doyle's/Holmes axioms have been grandfathered into logical scientific elimination Most famously: -
> "If you eliminate the impossible, whatever remains, however improbable, is the truth."

Together Houdini and Conan-Doyle confirmed the authenticity of the Cottingley fairies. Harry was obviously still entranced by the paranormal yet vehemently against frauds and con artists. Mr. Houdini was a regular visitor to mediums as he was seeking closure on the death of his mother Cecilia Weiss. Harry became quite depressed that there were so many swindles taking advantage of grieving people. Mr. Houdini and Sir Conan-Doyle invested a lot of time and effort into exposing these deceptive mediums publicly. Sir Arthur Conan-Doyle claimed that Houdini was more psychic than he was willing to admit and the two played off the media with their supposedly opposing viewpoints whilst remaining firm friends.

Houdini and Margery the Medium with members of Scientific American

In 1922, Lady Conan-Doyle, Sir Arthur's wife, a non-auditory medium, gave Houdini a message from his mother. Harry confirmed that he was emotionally moved. However, as Lady Conan-Doyle could not hear spirit, it did not contain the secret contact word prearranged between son and mother before her death in 1913, which was "forgive."

The Skeptics Pay Up
The Houdinis received this word twice from mediums. Once from Mina "Margery" Crandon, the wife of a wealthy Boston surgeon, whose lack of interest in personal monetary reward saw her become well known as a

medium. He was so shocked by this that he volunteered to serve as a member of the committee appointed by Scientific American to investigate her. Scientific American posted a $2500 reward if Margery's talents could not be disproved. Harry Houdini put up a further $5,000 of his own money that was held in Boston town hall as a bond that Margery would receive if he was unable to disprove her abilities. Unfortunately, it proved impossible for Houdini to be an impartial judge, he was later accused of tampering with evidence, and in his eagerness to prove her a fraud he severely damaged his own credibility by publishing a libellous pamphlet ahead of the Scientific American findings that saw him brought up on defamation charges.

Scientific American announced that its findings were inconclusive and because of his misconduct, it was ruled that Houdini's bond was forfeit to Margery. She donated it to charity. In light of this, the investigation into Margery was called to a halt. Yet, this incidence seemed to strengthen Houdini's belief in the possibility of communication from the other side and he and Margery somehow remained friends as it all proved to be one huge publicity generator for Houdini.

It is because Houdini had to pay this forfeiture, that modern skeptic associations take the opposite stand of putting up the money to prove psychic abilities on their terms whilst ignoring the plethora of positive results from true scientific studies into these phenomenon. How can someone who does not want to have any practical understanding of the dynamics involved set any sort of effective testing? Yet there have been many studies done, too many to list them all in this publication, the by the open minded and reputable, including Nobel Prize winners and top universities, proving in the affirmative. We will examine some of these in the chapter on Healing.

Skeptical Hysteria

A work of semi-fiction, "The Secret Life of Houdini" published in 2006 presents an account of letters from Margery's husband to Conan-Doyle stating that he believed that revenging spirits would soon kill Houdini for hiding the truth. It is a sad fact that Houdini died not long after the purported date of the letters, yet, is easy to be an accurate prophet 82 years after the historical event. Eerily, Harry Houdini died on 31st October (Halloween) 1926 from peritonitis secondary to a ruptured appendix as a result of a stunt gone wrong. A student, J. Gordon Whitehead, delivered multiple blows to Houdini's abdomen. This was a regular press trick in which Houdini displayed his abdominal strength however, he was not ready for the blows on this occasion and sustained injury. After thorough investigation by Mr. Houdini's life insurance company, his death was ruled an accident and no fowl play was involved. Nonetheless, it is sad that the media continues to be used as an involuntary tool of imaginary antagonism between skeptics and psychics.

Just one year after the book was released a claim was made that Houdini's body would be exhumed in 2007 to look for evidence that "Houdini was poisoned by Spiritualists," as purported in that work of semi-fiction. The family opposed the application and suggested it was a publicity ploy for the much-fictionalized book. This was later shown to be correct. Yet, a brief examination of the facts was all that was needed to show that this could not have happened. Unfortunately, it is this kind of stunt that prevents genuine skeptics and psychics from again standing together. Before his death Houdini declared: "My brain is the key that sets me free." More thought and less hysteria would allow both sides to work together for public good.

Harry Comes Back From The Grave

On his deathbed, Houdini declared that he would try to send a prearranged message to his wife, Bess from beyond the grave in a secret two-word code message known to no one else. A reward of $10,000 was again offered to anyone who could successfully deliver the message. Fifteen months after his death, on Feb 8, 1928, the Spiritualist Church minister, and medium, Arthur Ford, American medium and founder of the International General Assembly of Spiritualists, received a short message from Houdini's mother, and for the second time

"My Two Sweethearts" Houdini with his mother and wife, 1907.

the word "forgive," which had not been published prior to this event, was delivered to a Houdini. The reading was not for Bess Houdini, rather it came through when Ford was giving a reading for a small group of friends. This however put him in contact with Bess and after a further 11 months, on Monday, January 7, 1929, during a séance at the Knickerbocker Hotel, Arthur Ford gave Bess Houdini a two-word message, "Rosabelle believe." This was spelled out in a complex code devised and known only by the Houdinis for an early mind-reading act. "Rosabelle" was a favourite song that Bess sang for Harry.

Other messages were also delivered to Bess in a very theatrical Houdini style. Bess Houdini signed a hand written statement that Ford was correct. Three others present witnessed this. See fig.1.

Arthur Ford

One week later, in response to detractors, Mrs. Houdini wrote an impassioned letter to the New York Times and the New York Graphic, "stating emphatically that the message she received from Ford was definitely the one previously agreed upon and that she had not revealed it earlier to Ford or to anyone."

She insisted that there was no fraud, as others had claimed. On January 15, 1929, the article states,
> *"...No one but her husband and herself could possibly have known the details of the code. Neither overtly nor covertly could it have been gleaned, she said. To this argument she clung,,."*

Fig.1

NEW YORK CITY.
JAN. 9TH, 1929.

REGARDLESS OF ANY STATE-
MENTS MADE TO THE CONTRARY,
I WISH TO DECLARE THAT THE
MESSAGE, IN ITS ENTIRETY, AND IN
THE AGREED UPON SEQUENCE,
GIVEN TO ME BY ARTHUR FORD,
IS THE CORRECT MESSAGE PRE-
ARRANGED BETWEEN MR. HOUDINI
AND MYSELF.

Beatrice Houdini

WITNESSED:
Harry R. Zander
Minnie Chester
John W. Stafford

Facsimile of statement made by Mrs. Houdini the day after receipt of the message. Witnesses: Mr. H. R. Zander, Representative of the United Press; Mrs. Minnie Chester, life-long friend of Mrs. Houdini and Mr. John W. Stafford, Associate Editor of Scientific American.

One Last Theatrical Message

Bess continued to hold séances on the anniversary of her husband's death. Her last official séance was held on October 31, 1936. This final outdoor séance had worldwide radio coverage. However, after an hour, nothing had occurred and Mrs. Houdini decided to finally let Harry rest.

Fascinatingly, as the séance came to an end, a sudden violent thunderstorm spontaneously occurred. There were a large number of lightning strikes yet no one was hurt but everyone in attendance was drenched. The storm only occurred above the séance location not anywhere else in the area. That is either a very interesting coincidence or the ultimate way to end a theatrical life of proving unusual phenomena and disproving hoaxes.

Answering The Modern Skeptic

Because the skeptics societies have had their roll changed from initially assisting the spiritualists and psychics to expose the disreputable, to one where they are now seen as merely those responsible for casting so many ill informed aspersions on psychic phenomena, it is necessary to answer some of the common misconceptions attributed them in a book that seeks to teach and explain these paranormal skills. You will find interesting facts that are often overlooked in these arguments woven into this text. It is my sincere hope that these oft over looked facts may help to turn those who have taken on the role of the enemy into our friends and allies once again.

> *"It has become apparent that our technology has exceeded our humanity."*
>
> Albert Einstein.

It is my dearest wish that if a skeptic examines a psychic that they may see how our humanity may exceed our technology.

Why It Works

The One

The top seven psychics in Australia were chosen by elimination from 1500 applicants, based on demonstrable application of psychic abilities, for a prime time television show. The show had a reality T.V. format in which the remaining seven were to be eliminated one by one until three remained. Then Australia's most popular psychic would be chosen via viewer phone votes. This person would be "The One."

I felt very exposed whilst I was doing that show. Television shows in the past have treated our abilities like circus tricks, often trying to turn us into clowns. On top of that, one and a half million viewers an episode judged my abilities. However, the crew and executives treated us with respect and dignity. They gave it a big budget, $600,000 per episode, and high production values. Though the skeptics had a few cautious swipes, the vast majority of the feedback was phenomenal. The public was very supportive. It was the highest rating television show on a Tuesday night; even out rating "Big Brother" with their special guest star Pamela Anderson. It caused a shift in consciousness. The public acceptability of all things psychic has become far more mainstream. It was a privilege to be chosen to participate in a T.V. show that demonstrated to a prime time, free to air viewing audience that psychic abilities do work and have a valuable, practical place in modern society.

It is ironic that psychic T.V. show was called, "The One." In truth, there is no 'The One.' We are all 'the one.' Just like the Buddhist at the hotdog stand we ask, "Please make me one with everything." Yet we already are! The Hindu Vedic scriptures describe psychic abilities as "Siddis," which arise naturally as a by-product out of practice of advanced "yoga" or "union." We are all made up of the same substance. The page of this book that you are reading and your hand are essentially the same vibrating energy. My youngest teenage son has been trying to tell me for quite some time that my head and the wooden kitchen table I am typing at are made out of the same material. Though I hate to admit it, he is essentially right!

There is no name for this primordial unifying substance, scientists know it exists but have distained to name it. The alchemists called it quintessence in their early writings. Modern scientists have proven what they are cautiously calling "Dark Matter" comprises 96 per cent of everything, but they are still not sure what it is.

Science Knows 96% Of Nothing
The Australian Skeptic Society was initially very keen to participate in the show, until we kept getting things unexplainably right. I was privileged to be the person to get the least things wrong on the show. My methods entail being quiet, becoming a calm clear pool of reflection and asking only specific questions to which I

get only affirmatives. I was told by the production crew when Richard Saunders, The One's skeptical judge, set specifications for The Little Boy Lost test, he used strategies from the children's game Battleships. He confided to Simon Turnbull, the head of the Australian Psychics Association and studio executives that *"..if anybody gets this right they really must be psychic..."* I ran straight to the little boy's hiding spot in three minutes and twelve seconds. "I'm not sure how she did it." Richard Saunders confessed to one and a half million viewers. However, I was told that the offer from the Australian skeptics association of a $100,000 reward for anybody able to demonstrate psychic ability, under testing set by their members, had expired that month and was no longer payable nor made applicable to the show.

Psychic Science
Psychic science has been employed in technology for years. There have been breakthroughs. There is far more being employed by science than the century old quantum mechanics. Skeptics feel very uncomfortable discussing quantum science. The skeptic dis-belief system does not want to accept quantum science, dark matter, and other cutting edge physics that have been publicly utilized for the last decade.[4]

Victor Zammit a retired lawyer of the Supreme Court of New South Wales, and the High Court of Australia, when discussing the plethora of legal proofs for these abilities, claims that skeptics *"...dismiss and destroy the new information, including scientific proof of some psychic phenomenon,...This skeptic cannot allow his lifelong deeply cherished beliefs ... to be proved wrong, to be totally incorrect. So this skeptic will use every trick, every bit of energy and every means to try to ... defend her skepticism and ridicule and viciously attack any positive evidence ... I repeat, all sense of scientific objectivity will be lost."* [4]

Psychic abilities exist and are scientifically repeatable. You cannot quantify some psychic phenomena in the same way that you cannot quantify the amount of healing gained from psychiatry, but it makes it no less scientific. Because some of the physics that accompany these phenomena are now explainable, does this make these abilities any less real? We will examine some of the scientific studies conducted since the 1970s proving in the affirmative for psychic claims in the chapter on Healing. The methods and the physics of these observable phenomena are being utilized in modern technologies. It is unfortunate that skeptics do not keep abreast of what science has to say about supposedly unexplainable phenomena.

In this book, I will teach you some time honoured repeatable methods, the results of which are observable both objectively and subjectively, so that you can personally utilize these abilities.

The movie "What The Bleep" showed that scientific advances are causing many mainstream scientists to re-examine their assumptions about reality. Five hundred years before Christ, Lou Tzu in the Toa Te Ching said:
  "The wise man unlearns something every day"
Rather than stubbornly refusing to change their ideas many are excited about the new possibilities that understanding psychic science presents.

"In science it often happens that scientists say, 'You know that's a really good argument; my position is mistaken,' and then they would actually change their minds and you never hear that old view from them again. They really do it. It doesn't happen as often as it should, because scientists are human and change is sometimes painful. But it happens every day. I cannot recall the last time something like that happened in politics or religion." Carl Sagan

It is very refreshing to see modern scientists admit that they have come to the point in their research where they now know enough to admit that they really don't know much at all and acknowledge, that for all of their technological toys, the universe remains a 96 percent unsolvable mystery. It is lovely to see them tip their hats to their very early predecessors and admit that alchemical theories of earth, air, fire, water and quintessence/spirit, may have been right all along.[3]

The Dark Side

Physicists now believe that only four per cent of the universe is made up of matter that can be measured by conventional instruments currently at humankind's disposal. This means that 96 per cent of what makes up the universe is in a form that has never been detected directly in a laboratory: 73 per cent is believed to be 'Dark Energy' and 23 per cent an enigmatic substance known as 'Dark Matter.' The twist is that nobody knows what dark energy is, and dark matter has never been seen because it emits no light. Its existence is inferred by the gravitational pull it exerts. This is why the outer arms of a galaxy travel at roughly the same speed as the dense centre. Yet, the question of 'what this dark stuff is,' remains unanswered. The all-encompassing "Theory of Everything," describing the universe and all its wonders, that physicists speculated we would soon reach, is looking less likely now.

This scientific leap into the mysteries of existence occurred in 1998, when astronomer Brian Schmidt published a paper on supernovas that concluded that the universe is filled with a dark energy that is causing galaxies to move away from each other at an accelerated rate. The expanding universe is sometimes compared to a currant cake rising in the oven, with the currants representing galaxies and the dough of the cake representing expanding space.

Astronomers working at the AngloAustralian Observatory near Coonabarabran in N.S.W. won awards for confirming this. Scientists have dubbed the force that is responsible for this expansion 'Dark Energy.' Dark because it fills the blackness of space and because it is obscure, unknown and mysterious. For millennia, Psychics have utilized this substance in order to perform their abilities. It is the unifying force that makes it possible for a psychic to be connected to everything. It is because of dark energy that nothing can be hidden. By dipping into this unified field of dark matter/ lambda/ quintessence/ akasha, all things can be revealed to those with the proper training and attunement.

Looking At The Past To See The Future
Einstein, and the 5000-year-old Hindu Vedas, both theorized that energy and matter are essentially interchangeable and indestructible. Schmidt and his colleagues understood that their observations would

change accepted scientific understanding of how the universe operated. In the Sun Herald on the 4th Feb 2006 he said,

> "I like the idea of a finite universe that has a life cycle that begins with the Big Bang and ends with the gnaB giB, but this doesn't seem to be the way of the universe." [3]

In 1917, Einstein proposed a form of this theory using the existence of a cosmological constant that he called "Lambda," the 11th letter in the Greek alphabet, to explain the force that kept the universe in a steady state. Einstein declared that matter was nothing more than a field of force and that any physical substance is an manifestation of these waveforms. Different waveforms make different forms of matter. Harmonic field mathematician Bruce Cathie states that:

> "Einstein believed that the 'm' value for mass in his famous equation, would eventually be removed and a value substituted that would express the physical in the form of pure energy. This would be a unified field equation that would express, in mathematical terms, the whole of existence, the universe and everything in it." [2]

With his unified field theory, he proposed that the cosmological constant was a force that exerted negative pressure. Though the skeptics derided him at the time, eighty-five years later he has been proved correct. [3]

Quantum Mechanics

It took about 130 years before scientists grasped the counter-intuitive world of quantum physics in which the observer influences the behaviour of subatomic particles that are inherently unpredictable.[3] Yet it is via quantum mechanics we are the closest we have ever been to a scientific explanation of why psychic abilities work. Once this principle of basic quantum mechanics is understood, it is easy to grasp how psychic abilities can be possible. It is by the direction of attention and intention that the skilled and trained psychics can sift through the vast amount of information contained in the dark matter and find the specific particle of information that is needed to answer the questions asked of them. They attract the needed information and can thereby tap into a vast body of information and possibilities. This means a skilled psychic can see and influence the future outcomes. It is not just a passive reading it is also an act of skill and will.

Ancient Mysteries = Modern Science
Ancient mystery traditions have expressed this value, now represented as "Λ," meaning the lambda force, in a way that modern physicists were previously unwilling to examine. The Pythagoreans postulated on forces and particles smaller than an atom, 500 years before Christ. The Taoists before them called the all pervading, intangible substance from which all forms spring, the Tao, a seemingly the identical concept we have today in Lambda, and dark matter. Thousands of years before that, the Hindu Vedic scientist called the dynamic dancing dark energy Shiva and described his counterpart Brahmin as the force behind everything that joined all things together. Celtic mythology called it the Silver Net.

  A rose by any other name is still a rose and ancient theories are no less scientific because they are expressed in a different form from what is now the norm.

An alternative theory calls the unknown force that is causing the universe's expansion Quintessence. In ancient Greece, Egypt, India, South America and Asia it was believed that the world was made up of earth, water, air, fire and quintessence, a sublime fifth element. Western Alchemists, who were the predecessors of our modern scientists, took up these theories much later. In their own way, all of these ancient theories agree that this quintessential substance not only exerts negative pressure, but also has the capacity to change over time. These theories have been supported with the supernova data. Theoretically, at least, this means the nature of quintessence could also change in order to bring about the renewal of the universe at some future date as stated most memorably in the Hindu Vedas and ancient Mayan, Inca and Aztec writings.

Methods Preserved In The Mystery
As Katherine Kizilos, science editor of the Sydney Morning Herald reporting on this discovery said:
"...for us, the advent of dark energy marks the official return of mystery to its traditional place at the centre of the universe. You do not have to be a physicist to appreciate that where mystery lurks, awe and wonder are not far behind." [3]
Yet, for me psychic abilities have always been part of my everyday mundane existence.

o   Psychic abilities are not supernatural.

They are as real and as natural as all the other everyday miracles we take for granted. There is science and method to them. These abilities are repeatable and objectively observable. Psychiatry, which is now considered a science, cannot be objectively observed nor always exactly repeated. Psychics too are dealing with the deep human psyche. Science now embraces the rediscovery of the scientific principles that apply to these abilities. Yet, we really don't need to bother with scientific theory to learn this stuff.

The skeptics demand, "If psychic abilities are real how do they work?" Yet, I doubt that any of them can comprehensively explain how television works, beyond pushing the 'on' button on their remote controls. However, that does not make it any less real. It is based on liquid crystal technology and invisible 'vibes' in the air. Psychic abilities are structured in a very similar way.

Human Crystal Radio Sets
A psychic picks up information the same way that a TV set or radio does. A psychic could be described as a human crystal radio set.

Crystals used in radio sets

The science behind this is easily explained. Crystal radios do not run on an external power source. They use a crystal detector to attract, tune and convert a signal, in this case radio waves back to sound electricity. The detector is made from a natural or synthetic rock crystal in a holder. Earphones convert the electricity to sound you can hear. It is fact and physics that certain crystals can be an open channel to a broad range of frequencies and resonances.

Crystal radios can be designed to receive almost any radio frequency since there is no fundamental limit on the frequencies the crystals will receive. Crystal radios can receive spark signals as low as 20 kHz and below.

Although crystal radios are designed to detect AM, they also frequently detect FM, which is in the 100 MHz range.

A crude crystal set can be made from a coil of salvaged wire, a rusty razor blade, and a pencil's graphite for a diode. By lightly touching the pencil lead to spots of blue on the blade, or to spots of rust, they form what is called a point contact diode and the rectified signal can be heard on earpieces. How much more can a trained complex human receiver pick up when aided by crystals?

Crystals
Psychics often use crystals to help enhance this fine-tuning of more subtle signals and energies, thus becoming a sensitive human receiving instrument. Esoteric people feel drawn to crystals. Is it just a superstition?

Crystal silicon's ability to access and store information has had a great impact on the modern world's economy and lifestyle because of the development of crystal silicon wafers being used in the manufacture of devices such as transistors, integrated circuit boards and computer chips.

There are no techniques necessary to a psychic's use of a crystal. Simply having it in your presence or touching it or touching it to an object to be read is often enough. Holding a crystal close to the middle of the forehead between the eyebrows is sometimes useful. Personally, I will often use specific crystal earrings as a form of psychic antenna during readings.

Choosing a crystal is an instinctual thing. If you are meant to work with crystals, you will find yourself drawn to one. In fact, it can be a mutual attraction. Dr. Harry Oldfield, an honorary Professor of complementary medicine in many universities around the world and a Fellow of the Royal Microscopical Society is a scientist and inventor who have developed a form of polarized light photography that captures energy fields utilizing the special properties of crystals. His inventions have been used in hospitals, clinics, and private practices in Great Britain, Europe, India, China, Australia, North America, and Canada with remarkable results. His work is demonstrating that crystals have individual intelligences that chose to work with their owners. In the simplest terms, the work they do is to act as an energy tuner. The human organism has an unlimited capacity to receive information through the five senses, represented by the five-pointed star, and via input, that science, at present, does not fully understand. However, it works on principles that are long established scientific facts like the crystal radios and other modern technologies.

Psychic Technologies
Using this information along with the simple crystal radio theory, N.T.T., the Japanese communications giant, has recently developed a technology called RedTacton, which it claims can send data over the surface of human skin at speeds of up to 2Mbps, the equivalent of a fast broadband data connection. Though this method has been used esoterically for millennia, your own mind and body could soon be the key enabler of mundane data exchanges with other people, communication devices and in some cases with components within the body.

In this form of technology, a transmitter is attached to a portable device, such as an MP3 player, which then uses the human auric field to send data to another receiving device as long as they are on or within a twenty-centimetre distance from your body. The transmission is achieved by minutely modulating the electrical body field in the same  way that a radio station wave is modulated to carry broadcast data. This description is similar to the way that psychics describe what happens to them when they use crystals to amplify and receive data from another human or the surrounding environment. Interestingly enough, Japanese telecom is not the first company to utilize the human body as a vehicle for data transmission. IBM pioneered research in this area in 1996 with a system that could transfer small amounts of data at very low speeds, and then, last June, Microsoft was granted a patent for "a method and apparatus for transmitting power and data using the energy around the human body."

Psychics, without the use of technology, demonstrate that crystals can be used as tuners for the complex human instrument, and can amplify the resonance of these fields, which they then attempt to interpret.

Mind Reading Machines

Skeptics can no longer argue that picking up another's thought and feelings are unscientific. A first-generation commercial brain-computer interface (BCI) was commercially released by Emotiv Systems last year. A simple version of this technology that reads your mind to paint with images is on display in Questacon, The National Science and Technology Centre in Canberra, Australia, and in the London Museum of Science where it is used to push an electronic quoit around a two-player gaming table. It is called "Mind Switch." This technology was developed at the University of Technology, Sydney and has application for people with disabilities. It has been applied to control model cars and TVs by remote control using brain waves. We are talking hands free remote control. It can also be applied in a different way to monitor fatigue and give warnings before accidents occur.

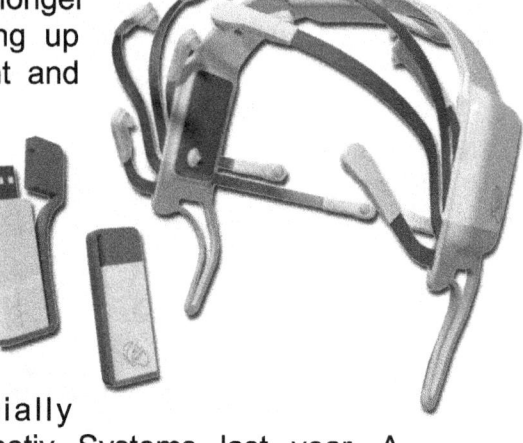

As early as 1975 Omni Magazine reported machines that could record and reinterpret dreams in their entirety. In the early eighties, the U.S. military's "Project Stargate" psychic spying program began to employ the Hemi-Sync machine to enhance and control psychic abilities. The Sony Corporation developed a Dream Machine in 1996 for reading and recording images generated in the human mind whilst dreaming. Then it developed its own much discusses version of a psychic enhancement technology called The Sony Psi Machine. Until recently, Sony had a whole research division devoted to technologies employing psychic abilities.

Images read from the mind of a cat have already been recorded from cats wired to electrodes by researcher Garrett Stanley. Fig 3 shows some of the images obtained.

Fig 3.

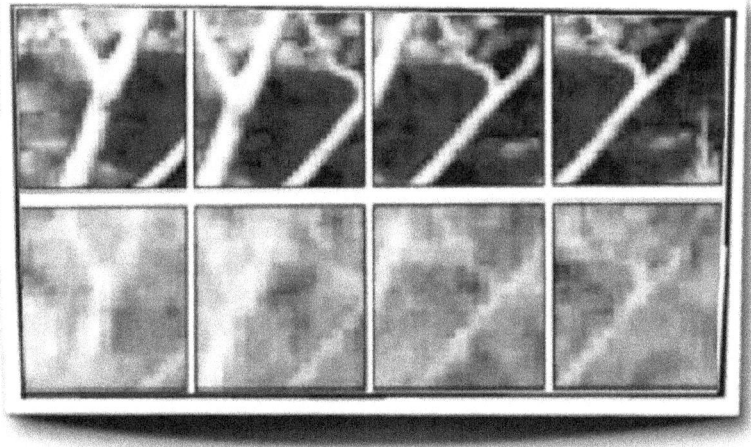

The next steps will be to increase the resolution, add monitoring of emotions, sounds, and smells. Then the technologies will begin to come close to copying rudimentary naturally occurring psychic abilities. I wonder what the skeptics will find to doubt then.

My Task As A Teacher
It is not my task to teach you physics. I have studied physics, engineering and architecture but this instruction

manual is not about those things. This is about other things I have studied. I am not a physicist, and it should be remembered that neither are the majority of skeptics. Yet, many of the greatest physicists of all time believed in these abilities. Pythagoras was a philosopher and magician as well as a mathematician; Albert Einstein believed he channelled his mathematical inspiration through his genii and dreams. Newton wrote more books on magic and religion than physics. The list goes on indefinitely. The skeptics of their day persecuted many great minds for want are now accepted as scientific proofs and theories. Historically, great intelligence believed in and taught supposedly unexplainable phenomena.

The truth is I do not know why these abilities work but I can teach you how to do them. We don't need to know the $E=mc^2$ to rub sticks together to make fire nor do I need to teach you chemistry in order to bake a cake. I can teach you the repeatable methods needed to produce these results. It is like dancing, everyone can do it; they just have to learn the steps. Sure some of us will be better than others and not everyone will be a Baryshnikov or Nureyev, yet we can all dance and we all have some degree of psychic ability. Are the skeptics going to say dancing doesn't exist because some people dance foolishly? We have all had moments where our gut has told us to avoid a bad situation or our intuition has served us really well. We all have also had those moments when our instincts could have worked much better. When you know the methods you can turn your 'sixth sense' on at will and you have access to extra skills to help you through life.

What You Will Learn

I have been trained in the ancient indigenous Alti-Himalayan/Tibetan shamanic traditions by Kushog, an aged female Tibetan shaman resident in Australia, plus Hindu shamanic techniques by Abi Ram of Fiji, as well as European mystery traditions through several secret societies. All of these traditions have preserved these 'how-to bake the cake' style methods. The effectiveness of my methods has been demonstrated to millions on prime time television.

In this book, I will share with you some of these methods to enable you to perform in a controlled way seven basic psychic techniques of: -
- Seeing Auras
- Feeling, moving and directing energy
- Working with Spirit
- Psychometry
- Remote Viewing
- Medical Intuition
- Healing and remote healing

First, we just need to understand what a psychic does and does not do and how they do it.

Seven Psychic Secrets

How It Works

How it Works

The word Psychic is a relatively new word. It has only been around for about a hundred years. Before that we had to use the old words 'witch,' 'occultist,' or 'shaman' to describe people with paranormal abilities. The words Psychic, and its sister words Psychiatry and Psychology, all come from the Greek word psyche.

Less than a hundred years ago the burgeoning profession of psychiatry laboured under the same 'on the edge' prejudices that psychics do today. Today most skeptics have accepted psychology but not psychics.

The Greek word "psyche" is the word for both "the butterfly" and "the unconscious soul." This implies that the deep unconscious is the most beautiful and fragile part of human nature. Developed and consciously controlled psychic abilities allow us to peer deeply into the soul reflecting messages from the universe that our client most needs to receive.

Psychic development is just like developing any other part of your body: -

- It takes Exercises
- It Takes Practice

To build the muscle of a bodybuilder takes months. To continue developing to high levels takes years. The methods of physical development are easy. Lift heavy thing - put heavy thing down. Yet, each time you repeat this simple exercise, your strength increases. The same with psychic abilities - the more you use them the better you become at using them.

The other thing you need to do is to begin to trust yourself. Self-doubt counteracts intuition. Our western society develops our self-doubt to extreme levels. We begin by telling our children they are imagining things and then we proceed to believe those who tell us it is just our eyes playing tricks on us. The best way to overcome this self-doubt is to practice these abilities with others. As soon as your friends find out that you are learning psychic development, you will have no end of willing volunteers. You will suddenly become very popular at parties and barbecues.

- You Need Feedback

Feedback allows you to trust that the things you perceive are actualities. In reality, you are becoming a mirror feeding back to the client what is going on for them.

- Don't Interpret - Just Report

Become a psychic reporter. Just *give 'em the facts and nothing but the facts*. If you are given a vision of a heart shape, don't jump to the conclusion that this person is dealing with a love issue. Your client will give it his or her own meaning. Just report to them that you see a heart shape. It may well be that you are seeing their deceased grandmothers locket that they have lost.

Receiving information is one thing; learning to interpret it correctly is another. In the classical period, the young strong psychic oracles had a network of old experienced priests to interpret for them. Today we read individually. Individually we don't have access to the kind of support structure that existed in the temple of Delphi. Usually we perform psychic readings privately, person to person. Don't try to show off how knowledgeable you are; that is a trap for young players. Even very experienced psychics can make mistakes in the interpretation stage. That is where the skeptics jump on any little error. They don't challenge the initial information. The clear, calm, pool of reflection is never wrong. However, the interpretation often is. So just be the psychic reporter. Deliver the information you receive as clearly as possible. It is, after all, not your stuff you are dealing with. The client is in a far better position to give meaning to what you are reflecting back to them about their situation.

Interpretation is an acquired skill that comes with experience. When you are starting out, you don't have that experience. Experience is more than just knowledge of subconscious archetypes - it is the whole picture.

Everything about a person, psychically derived or just observed, will tell you something about them. The things seen combined with the things unseen provide a rich tapestry as a backdrop for the information you receive.

The study of Jungian archetypes and emotional anatomy will deepen your perception. In addition, a study of the images in the Tarot deck will greatly augment what you are learning here. The study of The Tarot is beyond the scope of this book.

Be Calm and Clear
In order to receive information accurately you must switch off "your own stuff" and allow clear space inside your human crystal radio set to receive information about them.

Firstly:-
- Learn to be clear and calm
- Then you can be an accurate pool of reflection

If you sit cross-legged on a hard floor long enough maybe, eventually, you will be able to force your mind to go blank as the bum goes numb. However, there are quicker and far more effective methods that you can employ to affect this. *Please practice the following exercises before you proceed on to the seven steps for the best results.*

Prana
Prana is the name that the Vedic sciences gave to the substance that joins us all and makes us all one. It is the vital life force in breath. When Marconi invented the radio, other scientist thought he was loopy for believing any non-tangible waves could be carried through the air and converted back to sound waves so that we could hear them. How could air carry anything? Yet, as impossible as this seemed at the time, this technology is now the basis for a vast telecommunications industry.

Similarly, Prana is carried through the air to be picked up, received and interpreted by us as sensitive human instruments.

Breath Connects Us All

The sensitive and trained human instrument can pick up almost unlimited information from the *Prana* in the air. As unhygienic as it sounds, with each breath we expel billions of molecules of air that have been impressed with our vibration and information about us whilst inside of us. Each time we breathe in, we are breathing in billions of these information charged molecules that have been inside other humans. Whilst in a room full of people we will be exchanging an infinite amount of information this way. A trained clear and focused psychic will breathe in this same prana, to whom it will convey its vibrations. When we become clear and focused, we can zone into specific aspects of this information the same way that a radio tunes into a station. So how can we quickly become clear and focused?

- The knowledge is in the breath
- The point of power is in the present moment

So, if we breathe deeply and stay focused on the breath in the present moment we become clear, open, and charged with prana. It is that simple!

The Zigi -Ten Breath Meditation

There are two traditional forms of shamanism that do not use drugs to achieve altered states of consciousness, Tibetans and Australian aborigines. My techniques are derived from practices in both of these esoteric traditions. All states of altered consciousness can be attained with meditation and breathing techniques. Drugs are not necessary. To use drugs or technology to gain an altered state of consciousness for psychic work is lazy and dependence forming. The US military get their psychic spies addicted to using machines like the hemi-sync which eventually prevents the psychic attaining these states via natural methods and gives control to the psychic's handler. I believe that each individual should be fully empowered and the use of drugs and gadgets steal your power.

The Zigi is a traditional Tibetan shaman meditation. Zigi means "Glorious Monolithic Unity" or 'The Power Of One Breath' in Tibetan. The concept the Tibetan words try to convey is similar to Einstein's unifying Lamnda effect or the concepts of the oneness of everything, but it has the added meaning of *'riding the windhorse'* and you will see why at the end of these meditations.

- Close your eyes.
- Fill your chest very slowly to the top of your lungs, which extend to about two fingers widths below your collarbone to about two fingers below your rib cage.
- Then without holding your breath slowly release until you expel all the air right to the bottom of your lungs. You may feel like you are about to cough. That is OK.
- Imagine breathing in through the soles of your feet.
- Whilst breathing in draw in all the joy and goodness the Earth has to offer.
- Whilst breathing out release negativity and relax more and more with each exhalation.
- As you breathe out, cross your eyes and with your eyes still closed look at an internal point between your eyebrows. Imagine that you are breathing out from this point.
- You will feel a zooming intensity, a focusing as you do this because you are pulling your pineal and pituitary

glands into alignment with this movement. This is called opening the 'Third Eye.'
- Do not hold your breath and begin the cycle again.
- Allow it to flow naturally.
- Repeat this natural cycle 10 times.
- Do not count the ten repetitions off with your mind. Use your ten digits to mark off the breaths without counting.

This process should take ten to fifteen minutes. When you are finished, sit quietly with your eyes still closed. Your personal stuff has become quiet. You have become the clear, calm pool of reflection.

How do you feel now?

Calm? Clear? Focused? Relaxed?

The Theta State
This clear calm reflective state that you are now in is the Theta brain wave state. The waking dream state. You have entered "The Dreaming." This is the place of spirituality and connection, the eternal now moment, a point of power, often described in Australian aboriginal spiritual traditions. This is the place where all psychic work takes place. It is a realm that you enter using the Zigi. This state of being is what traditional European shaman called the fairy realm. Here you may see and encounter spiritual beings that you normally would not. Everything that you focus on or wish for whilst you are in this state will come into your reality with surprising speed. So be careful what you wish for in this state. You are primed. This realm is real. You are safe. Nothing is wrong here.

At this point, your internal slate is ready to receive. You are zoning in, ready to consciously focus on specific information. Receiving psychic information is like staring into a deep, clear, calm pool of blue water. Images arise from the depths, at first indistinct then clearer. Allow yourself to be inspired, breathe in, and be filled with the Gods. You will feel light and floaty. For at least half an hour, depending on the individual, you will feel as though you are walking through a lucid dream. You will feel slightly disconnected from everything around you on one level, whilst feeling totally connected to everything around you on another. Reality will take on a different meaning for you. Do not watch the television or listen to the radio or answer the phone and try not to be exposed to the outside world while this state lasts.

Doing psychic work in a safe environment whilst this state lasts will bring fantastic results. With practice, you will be able to reduce the number of breaths it takes to reach this state. Eventually you will be able to do this with one breath. If your schedule allows, perform the Zigi on a daily basis, if not at least two or three times a week is good to help you stay zoned and balanced. It is by practice of this technique that you will be able to become the clear, calm pool of reflection at will.

Inspiration Is Breathing In
Prana can carry inspired knowledge and insights to you from the universe. You will be more confident about receiving information for others if you are confident about being able to receive it for yourself. Use this method to find a solution for a specific problem for yourself or others.

Inspiration
- Find a still moment and your own space, preferably close to nature and
- Perform the Zigi meditation.
- Become the clear calm pool of reflection.
- Listen with your inward ear.
- Do not make any thought that occurs to you wrong.
- Just observe your breaths and any thoughts that flow with them.
- Write down or draw anything that occurs to you or that you see or hear during the meditation no matter how random it at first appears. These often connect to make a rich tapestry.
- Be aware of any signs or cosmic coincidences, (like a phone call from a friend that you have not heard from in a long time or an incredibly annoying billboard truck that you just keep seeing,) which may occur during or immediately after you conclude your meditation. This will be a message for you too.
- A specific and workable solution will present itself within a very short period. The first time you use this method it may take up to an hour. With successive attempts, the period taken to arrive at a solution will decrease until finally only one conscious breath is required.

Mantra
Active meditation uses the mind to concentrate on something. A traditional method of doing this is to use a Mantra. The word mantra in Sanskrit means instrument of remembrance, power, and communion with the divine. Mantra is a sound meditation. It can be as simple as sacred sounds like "Om' or "Ah." It can be an affirmation

to attract, emotionalise and magnetise something to you or a spell to work magic, which really are the same thing! It can also be an ancient and powerful sound formula in any language. You do not have to understand the language to invoke the energy of a mantra that has been repeated with intent for millennia. However, I do recommend that you find the meaning of any mantra of which you do not know the meaning, before you repeat it. Research it beforehand so that you know what you are wishing for. Always be careful what you wish for, as you will receive it.

Words that are repeated in this way take on their own life. Words are powerful things, more powerful than we give them credit for being. We know that "the pen is mightier than the sword." Why? Because words are thoughts that stay. Thought energy cannot be destroyed because you cannot destroy energy. It works, moves and changes things. The material world was described as coming into existence because of words in many traditions. Words and material reality are joined together. Mother and child, one come from the other. Sound empowers. It moves things. It vibrates and raises the energy in matter.

I use several mantras on a regular basis. I intone, chant or sing them to raise energy to be used for specific purposes. The Gâyatrî mantra is supposed to be the first thing ever spoken from which all other things were created. The Charm of Making, which is an old Welsh charm to raise earth energy and The Kurukulla Mantra, as she is the granter of wishes.

The Gâyatrî Mantra

The Hindu Vedas say that in the beginning Brahma, engineer of the universe, is born on a lotus sprouting from the body of Vishnu. Seeing darkness in all directions, not knowing his purpose or identity, he vibrates in the ether. Turning his attention inward, he meditates on this. He realizes that the vibration is the sound of a transcendental flute entering his ears. That sound, the original Vedic mantra OM, when expressed through Brahma's mouth becomes the sacred Gâyatrî - mother of everything.

The Gâyatrî mantra is the oldest and most powerful of Sanskrit mantras. It is believed that by chanting the Gâyatrî mantra life will be full of happiness. The Gâyatrî Mantra inspires wisdom and intuition. The word Gâyatrî is made from these two words:
- Gâyanath – that which is sung, vital energies
- Trâyate - preserves, protects, gives deliverance, grants liberation

Sing It To Remember It

A mantra is an affirmation that can be used to create your own reality. The Australian Aborigines *Sing* things into being. When you sing something it adds joy or other intense emotions to the equation that can emotionally magnetize the thing desired and draw it to you more quickly. Unlike things that are just repeated verbatim a sung mantra becomes an accurate formula that doesn't change much when repeated. It is quick to pick up, lodges in the mind more easily and is remember most accurately. The difference between Chinese whispers and songs is that songs retain their shape.

The Power Up Game

After performing this mantra you will feel like you are buzzing, charged up with energy. You are now a powered up version of that clear, calm pool of reflection. This sensation is called *Windhorse* by Tibetan shaman. You have raised your energy to the point where you can ride it and choose the direction, just as if you were riding a strong but cooperative horse. You have added power. This is a spiritual horse that is as intangible as the air yet as strong and quick as a tornado. In a very real sense it was windhorse that carried Dorothy on her journey to and through Oz. This energy will carry you along to where you want to go. When you are empowered you can ask a mental question of spirit on behalf of your client or yourself and your windhorse will carry you straight to the answer.

Why 108 Times?

Mantras should be repeated multiples of 108 times. Why chant mantras 108 times? This number of repetitions is traditional and adds a level of formula to your spiritual practises. 108 is an amazing number mathematically yet is also deeply resonate number to the human condition and this resonance can amplify your results.

Here are just a few of these harmonic resonances.
- There are 108 pressure points in the body and many forms of martial arts have 108 moves.
- It is reflected in our solar system, and is intrinsic in astronomical calculations

Amazing 108

108 is both hyperfactorial

$$1^1 \cdot 2^2 \cdot 3^3$$

and results in the phi ratio

$$2\sin\left(\frac{108}{2}\right) = \phi$$

is divisible by the value of its φ function, which is 36.
108 is also refactorable meaning it is divisible by the total number of its divisors (12), being: 1, 2, 3, 4, 6, 9, 12, 18, 27, 36, 54, 108.

affecting the sun, moon and earth and thus us. The diameter of the Sun is 108 times the diameter of the Earth, the distance from the Sun to the Earth is 108 times the diameter of the Sun, and the average distance of the Moon from the Earth is 108 times the diameter of the Moon. The digits of this number add up to 9 i.e. 1+0+8 =9. The 9 planets of our solar system by the 12 solar months = 108.
- It is significant geometrically to both the Sri Yantra, the lines of which intersect 54 times, each with a masculine and feminine quality, = 108, and the pentagram the interior angles of which measure 108 degrees.
- It is a Fibonacci number that invokes the phi ratio – the natural ratio of creation.
- It is the number of Surat al-Kawthar in the Qur'an.
- Chinese astrology and Tao philosophy holds that there are 108 sacred stars.

So there is a sound significance to repeating mantra 108 times.

Chanting
Get a set of prayer, rosary or *japa-marla* beads that have 108 beads on the strand. These are available at any Indian grocery store. It is interesting to note that the word 'bead' comes from the old English *bebe* meaning 'prayer.' Alternatively, you can make a set of your own. The concept behind them is to mark off the 108 recitations without engaging your conscious mind to do the counting. Do this by fingering through the beads one at a time for each recitation of the mantra. Begin with the one larger bead so that you will know, without opening your eyes, when you have completed the cycle.

You may aid your pronunciation of the Gâyatrî by downloading one of the many versions freely available on the internet. Many modern songstresses from Cher to Alanis Morisset and Madonna to Fiona Horne have recorded versions of the Gâyatrî. The version by Deva Premal is particularly powerful and very easy to chant along with.

> *"Aum*
> *Bhuh Bhuvah Svah*
> *Tat Savitur Varenyam*
> *Bhargo Devasya Dheemahi*
> *Dhiyo Yo Nah*
> *Prachodayat"*
> ~ The Rig Veda (3.62.10)

The Meaning of the Gâyatrî
The meaning of the mantra, word by word, is as follows:
o *Aum* (Om)

The three letters of the sacred sound Aum represent:

A - waking, U - dreaming, M – sleeping.

It is also called prana, because its sound emanates from the prana (vital vibration), which feeds the universe. The Vedic scriptures says "Aum Iti Ek Akshara Brahman" i.e.

"Aum- that one syllable is Brahman"

It is the sum and substance of all the words that can emanate from the human throat. It is the primordial fundamental sound of the Universal Absolute. As with dark energy, the primordial vibration is sometimes also represented as *OM* flows through everything and is the space between the molecules -

"As veins pervade all leaves and all bodies, so Om pervades all sound. Verily all this is Om! Verily all this is Om!" (Chandogya Upanishad II, xxiii, 3)

- Bhuh, Bhuvah, Svah

The three worlds:-

Bhuh	Bhuvah	Svah
Body	Breath	Ether
Past	Present	Future
Morning	Noon	Evening
Earth	Fire	Spirit
Gross	Causal	Subtle

etc.

- *Tat* - "that" because it defies description through speech or language, the "Ultimate Reality."
- *Savitur* - "Divine Sun" the ultimate light of wisdom not to be confused with the ordinary sun.
- *Varenyam* - "adore / best choices"
- *Bhargo* - "illumination / right thought"
- *Devasya* - "Female Divine Grace"
- *Dheemahi* - "we contemplate / we grok it! / I got it"
- *Dhiyo* - "intellect"
- *Yo* - "who"
- *Nah* - "ours"
- *Prachodayat* - "request / propitiate / pray"

The last four words constitute the prayer by themselves for liberation through the awakening of our higher intelligence.

Hidden Mathematical Context

Rishis, Hindu wise men, selected the words of various mantras and arranged them so that they not only convey meaning but also create specific power through their rhythmic utterance. The Gâyatrî mantra is composed of a meter called *tripadhi*, and is known as the Gâyatrî Meter or "Gâyatrî *Chanda*" consisting of 24 syllables - generally arranged in a triplet of eight syllables each. The Syllables also have a numerical value that totals 108. (See the sub section on The Amazing 108, on page 46 to further understand the significance of these numbers.)

My Translation of The Gâyatrî

The vital vibrating force of the universe and my own breath,
And the triplet manifestation of all creation inside and outside me,
That is, indescribably, what it is,
Shining warm and brightly like a sun:
Draw me irresistibly to the right choices,
Just like great female power of attractiveness and love.
I finally understand intellectually that
I am a part of everything and all of you, all knowing and all wise
Gâyatrî, who birthed all and knows all, help me to remember this should I ever forget

Other Mantras For You To Try
- Om nama Shiva

Means, *"I honour the god within"*

- Ma em pad mi mo

Bön Po chant meaning: *"The treasure is the lotus wise feminine mother"*

- Om Kurukulla hum hrim svahah

This is a Sanskrit chant to the ancient pre-Buddhist Tibetan Goddess of wishes who will grant your wishes and give you power after you have chanted her mantra 20,000 times, which is only one round on your prayer beads to her per day, every day for six months! It simply translates: *"I praise the divine Kurukulla"*

The Charm
This is an extremely powerful and ancient Welch chant. On the net there is some talk about it having been written especially for the movie "Excalibur."[2] The phrase "The Charm Of Making" was first published by the Irish professor of folklore, Pronsias Mac Cana for other things. It appears that the British film maker Ralph Boorman consulted Mac Cana, looking for an authentic magic phrase to use in his film, and Mac Canna told him about "The Charm" to which he then gave his more flamboyant moniker "Merlin's Charm of Making" However, Kerry Kulkins, a famous Australia media witch, introduced me to a version of this before the movie was made.

This mantra was originally known as just 'The Charm' but since the movie, it has come to be popularly called 'The Charm of Making' or Creating. It has not been written down before now, as it was passed from practitioner to practitioner as part of an oral tradition. I am entrusting you with this in written form as many are unaware of its power and disrespect it. This mantra is a great sacred trust that we need to bring back into action at this time. It has been released into the public consciousness via the popular media but you still need to treat it with great respect. Use it wisely and selflessly. Be Warned! This mantra calls forth whatever power is needed to create what you want in this world so be careful what you wish for.

It should be repeated in the lowest tone possible for you, and as clearly and slowly as possible under the circumstances..
- Phonetic: *an:al nathrakh, urth vas beth ud, dok hjel djen vé*
- In Old Gaelic: *Anál nathrach, orth' bháis's bethad, do chél dénmha*

Closest English translation: *"Earth dragon's breath, power and secrets of life and death, the magic of creation."*

The Psychic Work Room
As you meditate, via whatever method you are using, you may find a doorway opening up in your mind to a special place, a perfect place where you feel safe. It can be a green field, a walled garden, a perfect room, a library, or your deceased grandmother's old kitchen. However you experience this place, it feels perfect and at peace. You can encounter this place repeatedly. This is your psychic workroom in the dreaming. You may encounter totem animals there or a spirit guide.

I arrive at mine in meditation by travelling down a long dark tunnel that is lit indirectly and sparsely. I float on a barge down this tunnel until it opens up into a huge cavern that is well lit by candles and lined with old bookcases that are crammed full of ancient manuscripts. There is one table and two chairs. The table is very big and solid, like an old monastery table. On that table is an open book, a quill in an inkpot, and a skull that has a candle burning on it. If I need to know something, anything, I go to the bookcase and take down an old tome and there is the information I need. I copy it and place the piece of paper with the needed information on it into my clothes next to my heart. Sometimes a large male figure is at the table bent over the book he is studying, seated with his back towards me as I approach. The figure is dressed in a long robe like a Franciscan monk, or for that matter similar to what a magician might wear. He feels my presence and stops what he is doing and slowly turns to me. He rises to his full height; he is very tall, with arms outstretched in a greeting. We embrace. He always greets me with such love and warmth that I cry. He protects me. I am safe here.

Your psychic workroom will be unique to you. Nothing is wrong there. Nothing can be wrong here. You are safe and protected. Nothing can enter this space with out your expressed permission or request. Try to be aware of and take note of everything no matter how insignificant the detail, whilst you are there. It helps to keep a journal and write down any striking experiences that you have whilst you are there.

Lessons For Psychic Skills
Ready to begin lessons for the development of seven psychic skills?

No, the lessons in the seven abilities have not started yet. Now that we have gone through the preliminaries, and laid the necessary foundations, it is time to begin learning the seven abilities.

Each skill builds upon the previous one so follow them through in order.

These exercises are simple but they still require practise and feedback. The more you practise the stronger your abilities will become. The more feedback you get the more you will trust yourself. So let's begin by learning to see auras.

Seven Psychic Secrets

Skill 1

Seeing Auras

Skill 1
How to See Auras

Beginning to see auras is easy. Everyone can see auras; many people just don't know what they are looking for. We have seen them all of our lives but, at some point in our childhood, we begin to believe the people who tell us that we are seeing things. We convince ourselves that we are imagining things. So to begin to see auras again we just have to remind ourselves what to look for.

Remembering
Most psychic abilities are a matter of remembering. It is instinctive. They are part of what it means to be human, empathetic, caring, compassionate and helpful. It is the opposite of competition. As your psychic abilities come to the fore there is a drive to assist others. When babies are born, the doctors check whether it is a boy, a girl, or a psychic and if it is a psychic, they remove the competition gland.

The function of a psychic is to assist others. Your abilities are triggered by human need. That is when they will flow the best. Sure, there is limited effectiveness for the idly curious. Nevertheless, your abilities are not circus tricks. That was the hardest thing about performing psychic abilities on demand for the T.V. show, that psychic abilities limited effectiveness for pretend test scenarios. They work best when there is a real need. The tests had to trigger something in me, which some did. When I found the little boy lost in three minutes it triggered my motherly instincts and linked into a time when my own son had been kidnapped. Don't worry, I eventually found my son and got him back safely.

Living In A Larger World
We often limit ourselves, by choice, to living the smallest version of our lives that we can. Society teaches us to live under an imaginary glass ceiling, like fleas in a flea circus, afraid that if we jump too high we will bang our heads. Eventually we do not give our self-imposed limitations a thought. We begin to believe our self-imposed limitations are real when the truth is that the real world lives outside our glass ceilings.

Our trained inability to see auras is similar to the story of "Magellan's Ships." You will have heard this amazing tale in your primary school history class.

Magellan, a Portuguese explorer, working for the Spanish monarchy, discovered spice trade routes to Asia. Magellan's return route from the Philippines was through the stormy and dangerous Cape Horn. This southernmost part of South America is now called the Strait of Magellan. Magellan's men called that place "Tierra del Fuego" which, in Spanish, means "Land of Fire," because, at night, the local inhabitants lit many fires for warmth. Initially the crew thought that these fires were lit by the natives, the Yamana, who were waiting in the forests to ambush the armada. This proved to be paranoia, as the Yamana had not noticed them at all. The following account is taken from Magellan's logbook dated Halloween eve, 1520: -

> *"...when the expedition first landed at Tierra del Fuego, the Fuegans, who for centuries had been isolated with their canoe culture, were unable to see the ships anchored in the bay. The big ships were so far outside the boundaries of their*

experience that, despite their bulk, the horizon continued unbroken: The ships were invisible. This fact was learned on later expeditions to the area when the Fuegans described how, according to one account, the shaman had first brought to the villagers' attention that the strangers had arrived in something which although preposterous beyond belief, could actually be seen if one looked carefully..."

How could they not see ships that were so big, so obvious, and so very real? How can we not see things today that are just as obvious? The answer is the same for both of these questions. People do not believe things can exist and so cannot see them. This is now a well-studied psychological phenomenon. Psychologists call this phenomenon *"inattentional blindness."* It is the way in which prior beliefs, interests and expectations shape our pre-perceptions of the world and cause people to overlook the obvious. This was studied with laughable accuracy when a university staged a test of this effect during America's most watched football game, the Super Bowl. In the midst of the action, someone in a dark gorilla suit calmly walked to the centre of the field, waved to the crowd, and then walked off. When questioned later, less than one percent had noticed. Most of those who did were children under seven-years-of-age whose expectations were not yet fixed. When these children had mentioned the incident to their parents, the parents had told them that they must have been imagining things. Because of these blind spots, aspects of human experience cannot be seen objectively by those embedded within the Western skeptical worldview. That worldview, like any set of cultural beliefs inculcated from childhood, acts like the blinkers put on skittish horses to keep them calm, which after a while forget that their vision is restricted. Fanatics, including fanatical skeptics, suffer from inattentional blindness.

Similarly, with auras we have to believe there is something to see, then we can be re-taught what to look for.

We all see auras.

We can be retrained quickly to begin seeing them again.

Vision training is common in our society. Trained doctors can pinpoint a tiny blotch on an x-ray that a layperson would never have noticed. Similarly, I have a friend, for whom I have posed as a model, who is a photographer for a very large newspaper. Recently the paper swapped over to a digital picture format from photographic film. My friend has been trained to read negatives as part of his profession and has submitted his photos that way for the last thirty years. Now he has hit a learning curve and has to learn to view images and judge their quality in a very different way; in what we might have called a 'normal' way. He has to learn to see ordinary things again.

Children See Things
Children are not pre-conditioned and see the world in a very natural way. Fairy folk and so-called imaginary friends are as real to them as the corporal world. We all begin our lives being able to see spirit. Adults, because they have been taught to see things differently, say to children, "Oh, don't be so silly. You must be seeing things." Young children accept the adult's word as

absolute truth, without question. Well, OK, sometimes with many questions. The child will give up its line of questioning when its life support system, the adult, get angry or insistent. Thus, the child begins to doubt his or her self. The subjective and objective mystical realms slip away into the distance, and eventually can no longer be seen. They learn to see artificially and are taught that "seeing is not believing", because if their parent says it is so, it must be so. Sadly, they eventually totally deny their own senses. Thus, we lose the greater part of our existence and our world shrinks. No wonder teenagers rebel so hard against authority later in life.

Nothing Is Lost Forever
We can re-educate our sense of sight and learn to trust our feelings again. As children learn with play, if we *think of these psychic exercises as games, child's play*, it will remove any fear of failure and we will grow back into these abilities naturally.

Hands of Light Game
Here are twenty simple steps to enable you to begin seeing auras again. For this game, you will have to get up early in the morning as the sun's rays first begin to light the sky. This is a special time of day. There is a quiet stillness. The earth feels as though it is taking a deep breath. The Sufi's maintain that the hour at sunrise and sunset are when the angels, who are the guardians of day and night, change guard. Dawn is undeniably a high energy, uncluttered time, as opposed to dusk when, in an average household, the family is reuniting after a long day's work, the evening meal is being prepared and many personal issues of the day are weighing on your mind. Much of my esoteric work is done at the dawn hour

or at moon noon after all others have retired for the evening.
- Rise early when only defused light is on the horizon. (Check your local time of sunrise then rise approx. 1 hour before)
- Do a few minutes of basic Zigi breathing.
- Become the clear, calm pool of reflection.
- Begin to visualise your breath coming out of your third eye and your hands.
- Your face and hands will begin to heat slightly. This is called Tumo.
- Raise your dominant hand in front of your face towards the lightening horizon.
- Rest your gaze on the middle knuckle of your hand for about 30 seconds without blinking.
- Let your eyes go slightly out of focus.
- Keep your eyes open

What do you see?

Most of you will begin to see an outline around your hand. At first it will appear misty colourless or white like a ripple in a saucer of water. Then it will appear to glow a little like a white light around your hand. With practise, colours will begin to be perceived. Colours are rare and usually only seen during moments of emotional intensity.
Look down at your other hand and you will see the same effulgence around it and around your legs. Look at other objects; animate and inanimate. You will now begin to see effulgence around them as well.

If you have been practising this in the company of a friend, turn to them and look at their whole body. You will notice that the light and mist vary in depth around different parts of their body.

If there appears to be a break, split or very narrow part to their aura, mention this to them, and ask them if they have had any pain, injuries, or trauma to that part of their body. These can be emotional as well as physical.

If their aura is particularly large around any area of their body, mention this to them, and ask them if they have been playing sport or exercising that part of their body. (Or perhaps made love the night before.)

There you have it; you have just acquired the life skill of being able to see auras.

It's that simple!

Warning: This ability does not go away. You will not always notice auras but now you will not be able to unsee them again!

This exercise should take between thirty minutes to an hour to be effective for the first time. The time taken to see the aura/effulgence should decrease after that.

Being able to see auras is a very useful tool and there are many books and articles written on how to use it. Most metaphysical instruction books are determined to make the actual seeing of an aura for the first time a complicated matter, when it is not.

The same method is being used in Russia, in a project backed by Hillary Clinton, to assist sight-impaired people as the aura is detected in a different way to light waves. This makes it no less real. It can be photographed.

Your Own Spirit or Ghost

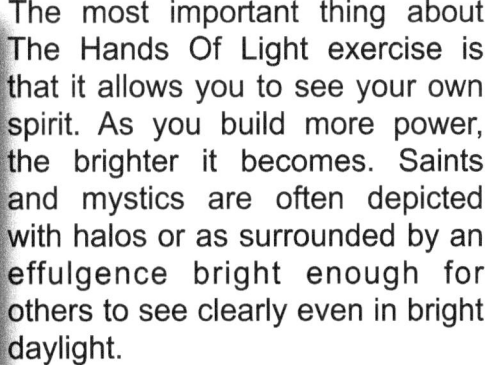

The most important thing about The Hands Of Light exercise is that it allows you to see your own spirit. As you build more power, the brighter it becomes. Saints and mystics are often depicted with halos or as surrounded by an effulgence bright enough for others to see clearly even in bright daylight.

You can see your own aura around your whole body.
- Sit in front of a mirror in a darkened but not blacked out room. You need some light to see.
- A dark background helps.
- Follow the steps for the previous exercise.

By practising to begin to see your own aura/spirit clearly you can also begin to perceive other spirit entities. My aura photo (right) shows some spirit entities, in, and emanating from my auric field that were captured on film. This picture and negative were tested and confirmed as untampered with and genuine by Gold Coast Film Labs in 1992.

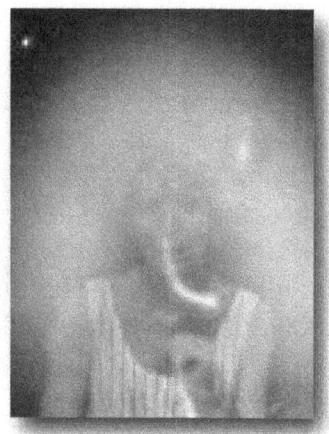

Aura Photographs
Having a good quality aura photo taken every now and again can be a useful tool for gauging your spiritual progress. Mind you, there are several methods for taking aura photos. Both of these photos were taken with what I believe to be the best method.

In a similar method to Kirlian photography, both of my hands were placed onto electrostatic plates. I then sat on one as well. Then, using a large camera with film sensitive to that type of radiation, the image was taken. Many new personal computer-based methods these days have only a heat sensitive pad which overlays the temperature around your thumb over a photograph of the rest of your body. Personally, I find the first method preferable.

Know Thy Self
Once you see your own spirit clearly and understand what you are seeing, like the doctor with an x-ray, you can begin to analyse it. Knowing yourself is the beginning of wisdom, like the inscription on the temple of Apollo at

Delphi. "*Know Thy Self*" meant that if they really knew themselves they would not have needed to go to see the oracle at all. Likewise, if we put the effort into truly knowing ourselves we will never have to go and ask questions from a psychic ever again! When you come face to face with your own spirit, it makes it harder for you to fool yourself. We get over what our ego and society are telling us what we should do, and we begin to see a clear picture of who we really are and what we really want.

Freud states that the ego is only the story we tell ourselves about ourselves in order to feel comfortable in society. In truth, the ego is just a romantic viewpoint of ourselves. The French word *roman,* from which we derive our English word "romance", literally means novel or *story*. The earliest of these romances to be translated into English dealt with themes of courtly love. These became very popular and were termed 'romances' and came to mean love stories. Therefore, romance stories are "story stories" are "ego stories". Stories about how egos relate to one another or *stories about how stories relate to each other.* I think we should stop telling stories to ourselves and buying into the stories of society and others and just see ourselves clearly for who we are and what we want and need.

There is nothing particularly romantic about your own spirit once you have seen it. It can show you without posturing, make-up or pretence how you really are and what you need to do to be all that you can be. In order to do that, we need to analyse what we are seeing. Where is the aura the largest and strongest around your body? Where are the splits or tares? In order for us to understand what we are seeing we need to know a little more about our subtle anatomy.

Dharana

Dharana means "visual concentration" in Sanskrit. It is a visually focused meditation. Concentration is usually thought of as something hard, dull and laborious but this is fun, which is why I call it a game. As a child I used to play this at school with a group of friends not realising just how much it was advancing my spirituality until much later in my life. It is my sincere wish that all children would learn to play such games at school. Before we begin this game, we must determine which is your dominant eye.

Dominant Eye

To do this: -
- Hold your hand to your nose, index finger pointing at a point on the wall.
- With both eyes open, sight down your index finger so that the point of the finger appears to cover that point on the wall.
- Close one eye at a time.
- You will find that with one eye closed the sighting will be unaltered.
- However, with the other eye closed the finger and the point on the wall have moved away from each other.
- The eye open when there is no movement between the point on the wall and the finger is the dominant eye.

Now we can proceed.

Mirror Game

- Be seated comfortably in front of a mirror so that you do not have to strain any part of your body to see your face.
- Sit at a distance of about three feet or one metre.
- Dim the lights, but not too much or you will strain your eyes to see yourself.
- Place one candle between you and the mirror, a little to the opposite side of your dominant eye, out of your direct vision.
- Using the gazing techniques taught in Hands of Light and See Your Own Spirit, gaze into your dominant eye.
- Do not analyse what you are looking at, just LOOK!

Don't blink or you will break your concentration. Don't let your gaze wander or you will break your concentration. If your concentration breaks, there is nothing wrong with that, just take a deep breath and re-focus.

If you can maintain your concentration for 10-20 minutes, some very interesting things will begin to happen.

- The features of your face may begin to appear to change in the reflection.
- Your face may become another person's face.
- Your image may twist and deform. If it does, don't be afraid. It will not stay that way. This is just revealing the pliable nature of perception and reality. Just observe impartially.
- Your reflection may suddenly feel much closer or further away.
- Your face may appear much older or much younger.
- The light in the room can grow darker then lighten again.

- This can happen rhythmically and repeatedly or slowly only once.
- The light in the room may take on a golden glow.
- The room behind you can seem to disappear.
- Your own face may seem to disappear.

Do not be afraid of any of these phenomena. They are natural and some are physiologically explainable. The results of what you see physiologically or spiritually are unique and will teach you intimate things about yourself. You cannot be wrong doing any part of this exercise, no matter what you see. It is all right.

Continuing the exercise, certain sensations will occur.

"Samadhi" Pants
You may begin to experience sensations the Hindu Vedas call *Samadhi* or "Mystic Union". That means, having lost awareness of yourself you feel that you literally become whatever you are concentrating on.

- You may have flashes of insight regarding a past life.
- You can feel that your reflection is something that is emanating from within you.
- You may feel a reversal of reality, that your reflection is the reality and that you are only an image looking out through the glass - like Alice in Wonderland.
- You can feel very alone and isolated from everything in the room.
- If you can continue for more than 30 minutes, you may feel connected to everything, a sense of unification with everything in the room. A sense that your reflection, the chair that you are sitting on, the candle, the mirror and the things not visible, are all

one being all apart of you and that you are a part of some much larger being. You may experience the sensation that moving any part of the whole is no different from moving any part of what you previously considered your own body. It can feel like you are in a scene from the movie The Matrix where eventually you realise that you and all around you are just energy that will move with your intention. This is the state we are ultimately hoping to achieve. This is Samadhi.
- Then your awareness can shift from your eyes to a drop or point at the back of the skull, as if something inside your head is watching what is happening, not your eyes. This is called called *Bindu* and it is the awareness of the watcher that is your true nature.
- From the Bindu point of view we are niether the thinker nor the thought, simply the observer of both. The audience for the play. The one who laughs at the cosmic comedy of it all.

It is great if you achieve any of these states of altered consciousness, or have any of these experiences. If you don't, do not get hung up about it, as this will only hamper your progress. Relax, go easy. Allow it to flow naturally. Whatever happens, happens! If an altered state is not achieved the first or second time, it may be because you are trying to force it. This technique is an allowing. Let it flow and it will happen eventually. Just keep having fun with it.

Do not underestimate this technique. Though it is fun, it is also very powerful. It is useful for developing many psychic abilities. The traditional Vedic word for psychic abilities is *Siddhis*.

Therefore, we are using Samadhi to develop Siddhis. That is why my partner calls me a Samadhi pants!

Chakras

The human body is so much more than what is seen with the physical eye. When you begin to sense the aura, you are detecting the human energy field or the H.E.F. The clear glow we have just distinguished is the etheric body or the energy that is generated by all other human bodies. We know that we exist simultaneously in a mental, emotional, spiritual and physical body. What affects one affects the other. The mind-body connection is no longer dismissed by science. It provides valuable insight into the nature of illness as well as the means by which the whole system can heal. Louise Hay's work has been largely responsible for popularising this concept. She has published exhaustive tables of correspondences between emotional dis-ease and physical disease. There is no need for me to repeat these tables here. Yet, any aspiring psychic reader requires a basic knowledge of them. For you to begin to read an aura it is suffice for me to outline the mind/body connection as it relates to the seven main chakras system.

The word *Chakra* means "spinning wheel" and is popularly used to describe the seven major spinning vortexes of energy in the human body. Chakras are spinning plexuses or balls of energy that connect us all to everything around us. There are hundreds more minor

Fig 1. Chakras by Johann Georg Gichtel 1874

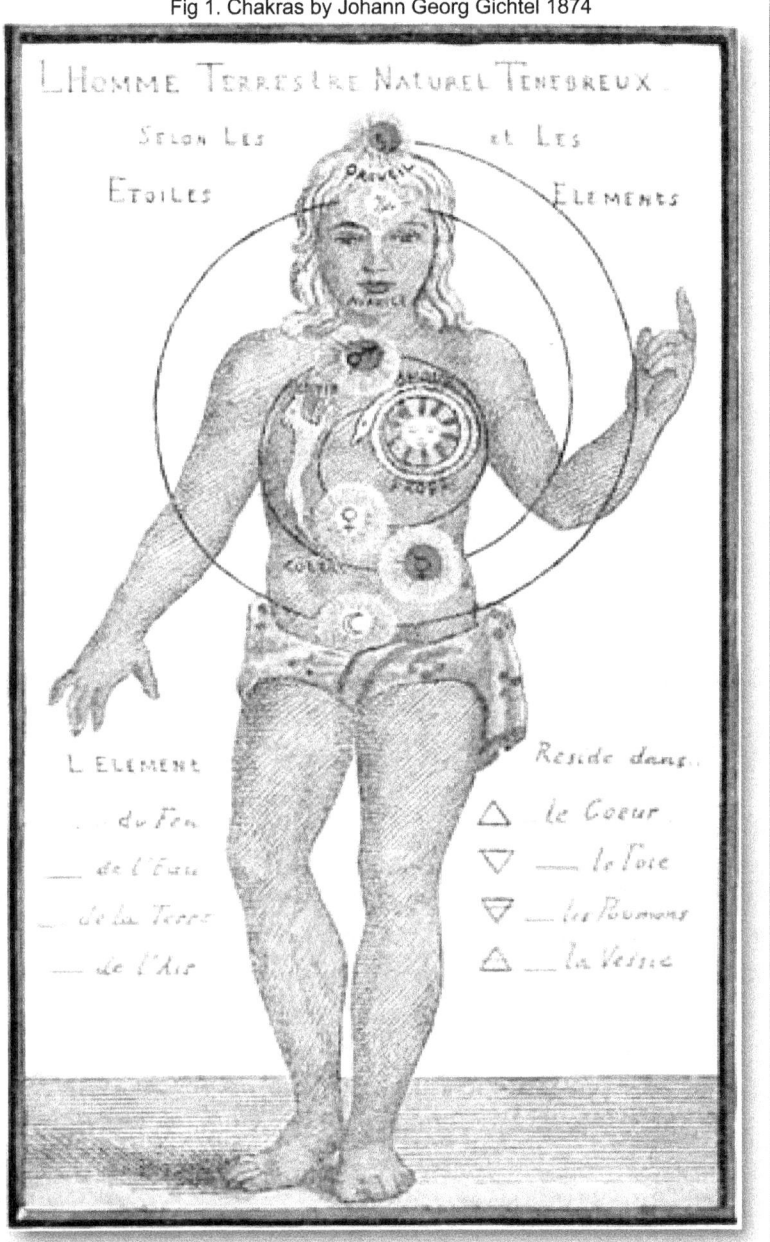

chakras throughout the body. A chakra has a front and a back like a funnel. The back of a chakra takes in energy from the universe, the planets of our solar system, the earth or any other giving source, so that it can be used in the human body. The front of the chakra gives out energy for our conscious and subconscious use. Chakras spin within themselves and around their heart centre as the planets both spin on their axis and orbit in our solar system around the central sun. Fig 1.

Seeing splits, breaks, flaring or colours in the aura over different parts of the body will correspond to this system and give you a basis to begin an analysis of what you are picking up. The Chakras correspond to the seven colours in the rainbow spectrum, the seven notes in the octave, organ systems in our body and areas in our lives as per the table on the next page:

Reading this information into your observations without interpretation is easy. For instance, if you observe a person who has splits in the aura around the head then they are experiencing or have experienced headaches and they are having issues with their crown chakra. If the aura is larger around the chest than anywhere else on the body, then they have a strong heart chakra and they are a very heartfelt and emotional person. Flashes of yellow and then black or nothing relates to the solar plexus and means that the person is in conflict. Sickly green indicates illness and will show up in the area governed by whichever chakra is not functioning optimally. If the aura is purple to light violet around their head, then their crown chakra is very active and they are a very spiritual person, possibly to the point of neglecting their earthly responsibilities they may also be related to royalty. A shape appearing on the forehead shows that individual is in the process of manifesting something new into their reality via their third eye chakra, etc.

It will become easier for you to apply the table of correspondences to what you observe in human auras with just a little more experience.

Chakra	Colour	Plexus	System	Disorders	Traumas	Issues
	Purple	Hypothalamus	Sub & Super consciousness	Coma Egotism	Beliefs shattered	Idealism Enlightenment
	Indigo	Pituitary Pineal	Brain Eyes Intuition	Migraines Vision impairment	Harshness Judgments War	Prejudice Incongruence Oversight
	Blue	Neck front & Mouth	Wind pipe Oesophagus	Jaws Teeth Throat	Inability to be heard	Communication
	Green/ Gold	Heart & Neck back	Circulatory Immune Rhythm	Chest Lung Back of Neck	Betrayal Rejection Cruelty	Love Empathy Emotional
	Yellow	Gut	Digestive Nourishment	Pancreas/Liver Weight/Eating	Power Self-esteem Conflict	Fear Security Conflict
	Orange	Sacral	Reproductive Elimination Cycles	Sexual Urinary Sciatica	Sexual Intimacy Support	Bonding Joy & pleasure Creativity
	Red	Coccygeal	Legs Progress	Abandonment Home-life	Settling Stability	Food clothing shelter

Seven Psychic Secrets

Skill 2
Feeling, Moving and Directing Energy

Skill 2
Feeling, Moving and Directing Energy

Q: Why does grass grow?
A: Because it intends to.

My son says the reason is *"because it has nothing better to do."* Teenagers!

Q: Why can grass crack concrete as it grows?
A: Because nothing can stop its intention.

It is by our intention we move all things.

If we intend to move an object on a table we reach out our hand, pick it up and shift it. The intention happens first followed by the resultant action. We intend to read this book and energy goes to our eyes. Without forcing it or even giving it much thought at all, electrical impulses move our eyes backwards and forwards across this page. If we intend to move forward, we expend energy to propel ourselves in that direction, stepping out and catching ourselves with our legs before we hit the ground. Step by step we move forward as long as we intend to. These things are so automatic. We do not even think about them. We don't calculate the kilojoules, and then do the maths to make sure we can do it each time before we begin. Many times, we are moving before conscious thought acknowledges the action. Conscious thought rarely comes into it. Do not try to rationalise what we are about to do. Just intend and observe the results.

- Energy follows intention and attention = Resultant action

Learning, as we are about to do, does require a certain amount of conscious effort, even though in reality we are relearning instinctive and inherent human skills. If you had an accident or a stroke, the familiar pathways energy takes in your brain may be destroyed, resulting in your engaging conscious thought to re-educate your body along new pathways in the brain and nerves to achieve the same result you have taken for granted since you first learnt movement as a small child. If you were to learn some new skill like playing a musical instrument, conscious thought is again engaged until the movements required become instinct. Learning to feel, move and direct psychic energy is the same.

Learning to feel, move and direct psychic energy is called Tumo. Psychic energy follows your intention in just the same way that the energy within your body moves hand and arm to raise a cup to the lips. Watching a baby learn how to drink from a cup reminds us how much conscious effort and intention was required to initially learn something that we no longer think about. Conscious effort is required at first until, eventually, you don't even have to think about the result. In the Kendo martial arts schools of Japan, they have a saying, *"Learn until you can loose the arrow without thinking about the target."*

An example of this was when I was asked to contact the spirit of an Australian Journalist believed dead. I sent out my energy, without expectation, to try and connect with him but the feeling of that energy was very much alive. I told my clients, the chief of staff of the Sunday Mail in Brisbane and her photojournalist friend Megan Cullen, to not give up the hope of finding him and to keep lobbying the government to intervene. Five month later he was located alive. Here is the letter Megan sent me:

> Hi Shé, My name is Megan Cullen and you did a reading for me on March 30th. We spoke about my kidnapped friend in Somalia, Nigel Brennan. You might be interested to read this article:
> http://www.abc.net.au/news/stories/2009/05/26/2580764.htm
> Like you said, he is alive, he has been shackled and his health is deteriorating... My Dad is ex-SAS and I asked his advice and he said he wouldn't be waiting around for the government to do anything. Well just thought I'd let you know this info (and that you were correct.) Thank you again for your help - Megan

Though the Australian Government did not intervene after repeated pleas from Nigel's mother, it is rumoured that Australian businessman Dick Smith, the man who originally backed the skeptic associations reward money, paid the ransom. To do this he must have believed. The results, by November are a happy ending as Megan describes below:

> Re: Kidnapped friend in Somalia
> Friday, 27 November, 2009 11:37 AM
> From: "Megan Cullen"
> To: "Shambhallah Awareness Centre"
> "Hi She`!
> Yes, it is such fantastic news, **and everything you said about his conditions, release etc...was true**! Your words always made me keep faith that he would be free...and now he is! I think he will be back in Australia soon...."

We all automatically perform Tumo to a certain degree until we TRY to make it happen. Then we get in our own way. The way children learn to get out of their own way is to play. As children, we learned to throw balls to each, hoping that it will hit its intended target. We continued practising this because it was fun and eventually the things we threw to each other would go where we intended. We also learnt to catch the ball and throw it back to an intended target. Likewise, this is the way that you will feel, move and direct energy by balling up energy between hands and playing with it.

The Energy Bubble Game
Sit across from a friend. Each of you will need to:
- Rub your hands together, generating friction and energy to warm them a little.
- Place your own right and left palms together.
- Push your hands together then release.
- Now, as with the Zigi meditation, imagine breathing out through your hands, this time stimulating the chakras on the palms of your hands.
- Bring your hands slowly back together, pausing when they reach approximately one inch or three centimetres from each other.
- Close your eyes.
- Become aware of the warmth of your own hands.
- Warmer as you move them together.
- Cooler as you move them apart.
- How far apart can you move them and still feel this warmth?
- Bring them slowly back together again.
- Notice as they come within inches of each other, a soft spongy resistance, like the gentle push you feel between the opposing poles of a magnet.
- Draw your hands slowly apart and notice there is a resistance to pulling them apart like a soft rubber band encircling both.
- Roll your hands around and feel a spongy bubble of attracting and repelling warm energy forming between them.
- Continue to imagine breathing out through your hands.

- With each out breath intend to increase the size and the strength of the bubble of energy between your hands.
- It will feel small at first but will reach six inches or twenty centimetres in diameter with surprisingly little effort.
- Play with it. Massaging it in and out.

It can take a couple of attempts for you to feel this sensation. Once you do, you know it. This is not a subjective experience, it is objective, and others can feel it as well. For confirmation of this, turn to your friend who has been doing this exercise at the same time as you.
- Place one of your hands between your friend's hands and one on the outside of their hand maintaining a distance of about 5 cm (3in) as if you were about to shake each others hand with both hands but stopped short.
- First either side of their right hand.
- Then either side of their left.
- Move your hands in and our gently.
- Play with the energy noting which side of the hand is warmer/cooler or exerts a feeling of more pressure
- Turn your hands 90° degrees so that your four hands form a box.
- Push out more energy from your palms.
- Move your hands in and out against the gentle resistance of the shared and contained energy that is spongy and warm between you.

What do you feel?

What does your friend feel?

Warmth, pressure, a tingly sensation are often experienced.

- Now both of you, individually ball up your energy between your hands as before.
- Push your ball of energy into your friend's ball of energy.
- Now both of you, at the same time, moving your hands in and out play with this combined ball of energy.

Now you know what it is like to feel and move energy around.

What can you do with it?

Being able to move energy around is the basis for all other psychic skills. It is used for all aspects of healing from simply making another feel good to sucking away illness, pain and negative influences. You will move it in and around people you are reading. You can send it into the akasha/dark matter to find information or specific objects. It can protect you by pushing other energies away from you or drawing to you what you need. You can create a large ball of energy to surround you that will act as psychic protection. It can be your psychic insulation that will prevent you from randomly picking up others' pain, emotion or information from strangers as you walk down the street. It can also be used as a filter to prevent specific energies reaching you. You can throw it over other energies to give them a boost or contain them. It can cloak and conceal, or conversely it can be used to make you shine and be noticed, depending upon your intention.

There are no limits to what it can be used for. The more you consciously practise and exercise this ability the stronger it gets and the more things you can use it for.

Now let's use some of this energy you have been moving around to increase your physical strength.

The "Unbending Arm"
This is a game used in martial arts classes. You will need a friend to play with as in the last game. If possible, this should be a friend of the same sex as you, of about the same height, and the same physical strength.
- Stand facing your friend
- Extend your right arm, palm upward and your wrist resting on the other person's left shoulder.
- Your friend places both hands on your upturned elbow and tries to bend your arm.
- Try to resist.
- You will find that your arm will bend quite easily as you have very poor leverage with your arm extended with your palm upwards

Before you try again: -
- Extend your fingers straight and flat.
- Lock your elbow.
- Take in a deep Prana-charged breath.
- Say the syllable Om. As you do so, visualise a steel blue stream of energy from the third eye to the heart that is flowing out through your arm, and shooting out through your fingers. Do this three times.
- On the third time maintain the image of steely blue lightning shooting out of your fingers and, when you

are ready, ask your friend to try to bend the arm again.
- Your friend will not be able to do so. It will not feel like you have to exert any effort to stop them.
- Repeat the above. Swapping around three or four times to prove to each other you are being objective.

This is the kind of power that can be released when you direct energy with your intention.

To prove to you that you are not imagining things, or somehow convincing yourself to pretend to be weaker on the first attempt, try this game: -

Let Your Light Shine Game
Most homes these days have at least one ordinary neon light. A small straight portable fluorescent tube works best for this but it should be the kind that connects to mains power. A very low electrical current makes the gas inside the neon globe glow, thus their popularity because of their economy. Some of these neon lights do flicker with the alternating current at a rate imperceptible to most. Through the eyes this flickering can affect the nervous system and has been known to trigger headaches, migraines and even epileptic seizures in some, so use commonsense with this exercise and never stare at a neon or fluorescent light. For the purposes of this exercise please: -
- Find a SMALL neon light, 30cm long or smaller, either at your own house or that of a friend.
- Make sure that the room is properly darkened, so that there is no light from within the room or without.
- Switch the light on for approx. 10 minutes.
- Now turn off the light.

- Now place your hand close to but not actually touching the globe and the lamp dimly lights, and the lighting is strongest near your hand.
- Now touch the globe and the light becomes brighter, although the current is still switched off.

It is startling the first time you see it happen. Yet this is a natural and powerful part of being human of which many of us are unaware. How does this work? Electrical forces are gathered, used and generated by our bodies. The stronger our natural electrical force, the greater our effect upon the neon light. Our brain synapses and muscular impulses are all consciously or unconsciously controlled electrical impulse, which add to this current. Added to this human body electricity is the static electricity generation gathered by your body. Static is not generated by the body, but simply by things passing over the skin. This knocks electrons from whatever brushes against the skin, or even from the skin. These electrons build up until there is a great enough charge for them to discharge across to something else, which we see as a spark. In normal daily activities, people can easily generate charges on their bodies in excess of 60,000 volts in an insulated state. Charges of 3,000 volts or more can cause sparking to occur. These events can degrade or destroy devices, erase logic or data banks in computers. Sparking can be extremely dangerous near explosive or volatile chemicals or gasses.

Disaster Avoidance Consciousness
This planet earth is also an electrical creature. The "Shuman Cavity Resonance" which is the measure of the Earth's electrical cycles, specifically the resonance produced when lightning excites standing waves between

the Earth's surface and the ionosphere. These occur at a rate of 7.83 cycles per second. This is close to our Alpha brain wave cycles when resting and our Theta cycles, (the empowering cycle we drop into when we perform the Zigi Meditation,) are harmonically slower. By synchronizing with these cycles, the earth refreshes us. If we are not in harmony with these natural cycles things do not go well for us and we experience the phenomena known as a run of bad luck or disaster consciousness.

We all experience disasters in our lives to a lesser or greater extent. When a person is in panic-mode their brain waves as recorded on an ECG mirror the waves that are recorded on a seismographs during an earthquake. If we are in this disaster mode we will be drawn to disaster areas. If we drop down into the more empowered stated we naturally gravitate to the empowering areas. We will be in the right place at the right time rather than the wrong place at the wrong time.

Disaster avoidance consciousness worked very well during the September 11 event. The miracle of the September 11 disaster, that has not been reported by the mass media, is that the total deaths from the World Trade Centre attack was only 2,792 of a potential 100,000 who are usually in those 2 buildings at that time of the day. Unfortunately 485 of those were emergency workers who entered panic-mode and rushed to assist. (WARNING - Panic-mode is contagious and it can lead to you being involved in disasters you could have otherwise avoided– Avoid panicked people, especially large groups of panicked people.) Which drops the figure of those that died that were in the buildings and the plane to an astoundingly low 2,302. Also it must be noted that of the 490 passengers on the Boeing 747 that hit the buildings on that day only 92 died. This is a miraculous, greater than 98%, survival rate. Over 98,000 people avoid their personal Armageddon that day. Yet this miracle was not mentioned in any of the mass media. WHY? Because panicked people are disempowered and easy to control. That is why the media reports more bad news than good to keep us in this low and disempowered state.

Statistics From September 2002
Source: CNN & Reuters

These resonant cycles pervade most things on this planet. A compass enclosed in an airtight case always points north. These lines of force are deeply penetrating except when something is insulated. Rubber soles on sneakers do not let us properly recharge our flagging batteries. It is no wonder that the first thing we want to do when we relax is kick off our shoes. Unless the conditions outside are freezing, we should try to have a daily barefoot walk on exposed ground, beach, grass etc. but not concrete or tar. If it is possible, time and circumstances permitting, walking an imperial mile per day (1.8km) whilst intentionally deeply breathing in Prana will charge you up to your optimum energy levels.

Bioelectric And Radio Frequency Generation
It is well known that large electric eels have an electric organ that extends almost the entire length of their body. The organ consists of hundreds of thousands of electrocytes capable of generating electric discharges. Study has shown that electric eels also have high-frequency sensitive receptors patchily distributed over their body, which are useful for detecting their prey. These eels transmit direction-finding pulses at a

frequency of 50 hertz and are capable of producing shocks reaching one amp and 600 volts.

Human Electricity

It is also well known that the human body generates an electrical current by changing chemical concentrations in and around the nerves. The brain is an electro-chemical organ. When a nerve signal is sent, potassium ions flood out of nerve cells and sodium ions flood in. The difference in concentrations inside and outside the nerve cell of the ions means that charge is created across the nerve cell membrane. However, these impulses vary so much with fluctuation in human activity that some claim that it has proven elusive to quantify, whilst others claim that the action potentials in nerve cells are quite well known, and are described very specifically in basic anatomy and physiology texts. The fact remains that every cell in the body is a microscopic electromagnetic device. Every chemical reaction involves an electromagnetic transaction.

Electricity, Nerves and Chakras

The nervous system not only conveys messages from the different parts of the body to the brain, but also serves to convey the signals, which initiate motion to the various parts. In short, there can be no motion of any part of the body without the electrical signals from the nerves and no signals from the nerves without intention.

The nervous system is a part of the great energy-producing system of the body, as much a part of it as is the brain. This nerve and intention-energy spreads itself beyond the limits of the body. The nervous system of the human being is a very intricate mechanism far more sensitive than any man made device. Like the electric eel, the main human electrical feature, the spinal cord, runs through an opening in the spinal column, this is directly connected with the brain matter in the skull. From the spinal cord emerge many sets of nerves, in pairs, which branch out in smaller and smaller filaments, until every part of the body is supplied with a direct connection with the main nerve trunk.

There are other large cables of nerves descending into the trunk of the body, apart from the spinal cord system, although connected with the latter by nerve links. In different parts of the body are found great masses of nerve-substance, matted knots or tangles of nerves. These centres are the plexuses or chakras we have previously discussed. Like the electric eel, these centres can also receive information from the outside world. The principal, the "solar plexus," is well known for being the major receptor of feelings about others via our 'gut' feelings. The solar plexus being our personal power centre will let us know if our safety is threatened by producing feelings of weakness and the sinking lead feelings in the stomach.

Human Battery Potentials
Naturally occurring stored and generated body energy and electricity for healing have been studied for years and the results are positive. Skeptics who claim that electricity does not occur in the human body for healing have not done basic research.

Measurements of transcutaneous voltage have been made by Dr A. T. Barker, Department of Medical Physics and Clinical Engineering in the Hallamshire Hospital,

Sheffield, England on 17 volunteers. The results show the presence of "skin battery" voltages comparable in size to those previously reported for amphibian and mammalian skin.

Biological cells and tissues are much more complex systems than physicists are used to studying. Eiichi Fukada of the Institute of Physical and Chemical Research in Wako, Japan, who pioneered this subject claims: *"The clinical applicability has been established... electricity ... is caused by both piezoelectricity in collagen and streaming potential in micro canals in bone."*

Wendell S. Williams of the University of Illinois at Urbana-Champaign says that researchers are still trying to understand these signals and relate them "to specific mechanisms well known in physics," yet clinical application of the findings is already happening. Williams remarks: *"It is interesting that biological tissues, which have been on earth for millions of years, utilise... displaceable bound charge, for generating unusually large electric fields."* [1]

The research of these gentlemen demonstrates that a very minute current, in the range of a microampere or one millionth of an ampere, can play an important role in the health and accelerated healing of bone and tissues.

This electricity is transferable between two living things by touch and intention in the same way that the electric eel can consciously transfer its energy. Trained psychics can transfer their energy to another for healing or another intended purpose as the above research shows.

- Becoming aware of your body's energy allows you to intentionally utilize its potential

Tumo As Body Heating

You may have read of the Tibetan Lamas and monks famous for generating enough body heat to keep them warm in the middle of the coldest extremes of a Tibetan winter. This is a well-documented use of conscious intent and control of your body's energy.

Tumo Masters In Tibet

To be considered a Tumo Master in Tibet you must be able to pass a trial. A frosty winter day on the shore of a frozen river or a lake is selected. To increase the degree of difficulty sometimes a moonlit night, with a hard wind blowing, is chosen. A hole is made in the ice. The examined sits on the bare cold ground, cross-legged, and naked. Sheets, the size of a large shawl, are dipped in the icy water. The examined is wrapped in one of them and must dry it with his body heat. During these trials the body heat has been measured to increase by as much as eight degrees Celsius, placing the examined way beyond fever pitch. As soon as the sheet has become dry, it is again dipped in the water and placed on the novice's body to be dried as before. The operation can go on in that way until daybreak. By then, he may have dried as many as 40 sheets. Nevertheless, drying at least three sheets under these conditions qualifies the examined to be known as a Tumo Master or *Respa*. This entitles those who pass to wear the white cotton shirt, a sign of proficiency in Tumo.

Another less sophisticated test of Tumo is simply sitting in the snow. The quantity of snow melted under the examined and the distance to which it melts around him are taken as measures of his ability. The word Respa literally means "one who wears a single cotton garment in all seasons". Yet, this is not strictly adhered to. Though the training is hard, it is still nice to be gentle with yourself in all things and sometimes rugging up by an open fireplace is one of life's great joys.

The Warming
Warmth and the giving off heat are outward displays of energy at work. Many people experience warmth whilst performing various psychic tasks. We would never ask anyone to perform something so dangerous to just to pointlessly show off. However, this skill has saved lives. The point of mastering these exercises is not so that you can perform circus tricks for public amusement, acquire a title or put on a futile display that only gratifies an ego that wants to be better than someone else. The point of acquiring these skills is so that you can become fully empowered and master your abilities and be able to assist others. Though we are having fun learning these things, it is disciplined practise will give you proficiency.

The Zigi breathing outlined earlier is essential to the successful completion of this exercise. Please practise Zigi breathing until you feel you have mastered it before attempting this Tumo meditation. Though you can practise this whenever you feel the cold, this training is best practised in the early hours, just before dawn.

The 'Heating Up' Game
Find yourself a quiet place. So quiet, if you concentrate you can listen to the beat of your own heart. Always sit with the spine straight. If you can, sit crossed-legged on

the floor in the full lotus. If not, make yourself as comfortable as possible so that you will not want to move. That is what cushions were invented for.
- Clasp the hands together under the thighs or buttocks.
- Push your stomach in and out a few times then give the body a good shake as you may be sitting still doing this visualisation for up to an hour.
- Begin by performing the Zigi meditation.
- Become the clear, calm pool of reflection.
- Then focus on your heartbeat again.

Hear the sound, feel the warmth, the rhythmic beating; the generous way it grants and maintains your life with each beat. Listen to the beat of your own heart and realise that the physical heart is good. It just is. There is nothing bad about it. There is nothing wrong here. In its rhythmic beating there is no room for emotion - positive or negative. Pride, anger, hatred and all distress slowly melt away with its rhythmic beating. With each beat and each breath, draw in blessings. These blessings warm you, relax you and fill you with joy. Centre yourself; dismiss all cares and conscious thoughts. You are perfectly calm.

- Visualise breathing each in-breath with your heart. Deep breaths focused with intention act as bellows to awaken the smouldering fire of your being.
- Each breath into your heart is warm; you may become emotional whilst breathing into your heart as this is stimulating your heart chakra.
- It feels like swallowing a very hot drink. The warmth melts into you and disburses through your chest flowing down to your stomach and out to your limbs.

- Intone deep in your chest the seed syllable "Ram," the mystic name of the fire. That sound is the seed of the element of fire itself. This is a *bija* mantra. When mastered, "Ram" correctly pronounced can produce fire or produce flames without fuel. Ram awakens the inner vision of your internal spark.
- At first you see your internal fire as only the size of a marble. Your heart is a small sun within your body and your lungs are the bellows that fan the flames bigger, brighter, and hotter.
- Each deep inspiration is followed by retention of breath for up to 60 seconds.
- With each retention visualise fire waking up and rising along the centre of the body searching for air.
- At first, this central artery of fire is perceived as the thinnest hair filled with the rising flame and fanned by the current of air produced by the breath.
- The fire artery increases in size and becomes as large as a little finger then it increases to the size of an arm. Eventually the artery fills the whole body, until the body becomes a tube filled with blazing fire fanned by the air of your breath.
- The body will cease to be perceived. Enlarged beyond all measure, the fire artery engulfs the whole world, you feel yourself to be in a firestorm, and then you are the firestorm that engulfs the whole world in a sea of flame.
- Each out breath is slow taking up to 60 seconds.
- Visualise breathing out fire like a dragon with each out breath.
- With each out breath the world is visualised as being filled with fire. Visualise the sun at the centre of every warm being and object.
- Visualise pushing heat energy out from your heart with

effort through the rest of your body.
- Force heat through your body with each out breath.
- To warm your extremities, visualise a small sun in the palm of each hand, on the sole of each foot and below the solar plexus. By rubbing the suns together, fire flares up and strikes the heart sun, and a smaller sun below in the solar plexus, which flares up in its turn and fills the whole body with fire.
- Push heat out with each out breath, like the effort taken to push a heavy load on a warm day, your temperature rises and you begin to perspire.
- Your face begins to heat before the rest of your body.
- Each in breath and each out breath make you warmer and warmer until you feel fevered.

The 'Cooling Down' Game
You are finally hot enough, you will need to cool down. Repeat these visualisations in reverse order.

- No longer push with your breath.
- Breathe easy, and allow each in breath to cool your lungs.
- Feel the coolness of the air carry away the heat from your body.
- The firestorm abates and is gradually re-absorbed into your body.
- The fire artery is reduced to the size of an arm.
- The artery decreases to the size of the little finger.
- Then becomes as thin as a hair.
- The fire travels back down the mid line of your body to be retained in a small orb the size of a marble.
- Eventually all sensation of fire disappears.
- Your body feels comfortable.

The more you practise tumo for body heat the easier it gets. When one begins the training, the increasing heat will only last while practising the exercise. With practise, you will find the production of tumo becomes virtually effortless and last for hours. My partner performed tumo for body heat quite naturally when he was a diver with the Water Police. He would use tumo to heat up after being deeply submerged in cold water for more than two hours to avoid hypothermia. He could remain submerged in cold water for up to six hours using this technique, which was approximately four hours more than his colleagues. For him, it became an acquired habit that allowed a pleasant feeling of warmth to spread gradually all over his body whilst doing a necessary but unpleasant job.

The Lifting Game - Levitation Exercises
Now let's do a very simple exercise using your newly acquired ability to feel and direct energy. This will instantly increase your personal power. You will need to find four friends willing to do this with you.
- One person sits upon an upright chair.
- The person on the right hand side of the sitter near his shoulders places his left forefinger under the armpit
- The person standing on his left places the forefinger of his right hand underneath the left armpit.
- The person near his right knee places the left forefinger under the sitter's right knee
- The person near the sitter's left knee places his right forefinger under the sitter's left knee.
- When all are in place shout out "Lift Sitter!"
- All will try hard using only the forefinger and find that the person is too heavy to lift.
- Let go of the sitter

- The four lifters put their right hands on top of each other and then each places their left hand on top. Resulting in a pile of eight hands
- With hands still stacked all four lifters take 10 deep breaths. All breathing deeply in and out together. It helps if the sitter counts these. The sitter need not take part in the breathing exercise.
- All lifters replace their respective forefingers under the armpits and knees of the sitter
- Then all four lifters simultaneously take a further three deep breaths.
- On the third count, the last deep breath is held and you shout "Lift Sitter!"
- All lifters make another effort to lift the sitter.
- Now you will find the sitter is actually lifted easily by one finger from each person.
- Continue lifting until the sitter is high up into the air.
- Lower the sitter gently and effortlessly back in to place.
- Then breathe as normal

What Is This Power And Strength?

Does the weight vary? The weight actually does not alter. The lifter experiences the world as being lighter. However, there is an increased force, which the people lifting acquire from their breath.

Experienced furniture removers use this method to move otherwise almost immovable objects without calling it levitation. You will have seen this game played in the Hollywood movie The Craft. In that movie they called it Light as a Feather, Stiff as a Board. Unfortunately, Hollywood, like all good illusionists, makes this ability appear somehow unobtainable, when this is a very ordinary force you can all tap into once you are aware of its existence.

Skinny 55kg Shé effortlessly lifting twice her body weight by herself, a 110kg Ken Wills

Then Where Does This Power Come From?
The power comes from the Prana. When breathing with intent the prana life force energy is conveyed to the intended job through the breath. It joins and connects us to all living matter so we can borrow some to use for whatever we intend. In this respect, it is similar to the concept of "The Force" in the movie Star Wars. You can

draw on it to supercharge yourself whenever you need it, as with the lifting game. Martial artists will teach the conscious use of Prana or intent with *Chi* force. When you ingest food, you are consuming the remnants of Prana out of whatever you choose to eat. That is why many aware people prize live whole foods so highly. Foods that are high in prana will give you a tingling sensation in your mouth, ears and nose as you consume them.

As well as drawing Prana from our food and the air around us, you can also draw Prana directly from the earth, as the earth is a living breathing being; the oldest, largest and strongest you have direct contact with.

Psychic Vampires
Many people in the west have not mastered the art of drawing Prana from the breath or from the earth so they become skilled at siphoning it off other people. You can easily identify these people:
o Attention seekers,
o People who want to control others,
o People who cry "poor me" all the time,
o People who always want to be right,
o Who engage in incessant arguments,
o Battered wives,
o Wife beaters and
o Troublemaking children

These are all what could be termed pranic or psychic vampires.

Psychic vampirism is an addictive behaviour that can be easily corrected once awareness is acquired of what they are actually doing to themselves and others as well as awareness that there is a much better alternative. Siphoning energy off people as a life style is like a starving man insisting on picking through the garbage bins of a restaurant, when he has a first class, all expenses paid invitation to an all-you-can-eat smorgasbord waiting inside. By making a life style of siphoning energy from others in this way, they short-change themselves into living a half-life that is filled with insecurity and manufactured drama.

There is a positive use for this ability; I have seen this ability used consciously by adepts to contain a particularly rabid personality forcing itself on others in public. This benefited everyone present. However, psychic vampires only want to benefit themselves by either playing the victim or victimising others. Because psychic vampires are tapping such a limited source, they seldom have the energy to pursue anything worthwhile.

Once an individual learns how to tap into the limitless supply of Prana from the air and the earth they can supercharge themself. If you learn how to supercharge yourself this way you will have enough energy to make *all* things possible. This is also very attractive and will draw other people to you. You will be aglow with spirit and you will wonder how you denied yourself this aspect of your own divinity for so long.

Children Need Prana Donors

Young children have a singular need for this life force energy that their mother and many others are more than willing to give to them. A healthy adult has naturally grown out of this co-dependency. Sharing prana with a small child is a very rewarding experience. Yet because we are freely giving our life force to a growing being, small children are very draining. It is ideal when a mother can share this responsibility with a loving trusted family. The mother can then have a chance to recharge her own Prana batteries with some deep breaths in her own space or preferably having time out and doing this at a high energy spot like the rainforest or the beach.

When an aware mother raises a child, it will naturally and easily make the transition to drawing prana from its environment. An aware mother will ensure that the child has time to itself daily, preferably when it is in contact with nature. Nor will she deride the child that stares off into space daydreaming and breathing deeply. For this is the time when the child is tying it's own thought forms to its breathing.

If this transition to independence is not made, an addictive co-dependant struggle for pranic energy can be set up between mother and child that will endure until much later in life. This cycle only can be broken when the individual becomes aware and empowered.

Using Prana with Conscious Intent
Whenever one takes into the lungs a deep regular breath and thinks of anything in particular, at that moment a link is made between the person thinking and the thing being thought of, and so the thought to some extent there and then becomes the object thought of. We can link to
- another person,
- spirit entity, or for that matter,
- an apparently inanimate object to be lifted.

With conscious intent and a deep Prana breath we can create a link to anything.

There is no time or space to prana. Within the Dreaming via Prana all things exist at once together. Your job as a psychic is to sort through it, using the conscious link to find relevant information.

Prana connects all things to each other. We are all *The One.*

Seven Psychic Secrets

Skill 3
Working With Spirit

Skill 3
Learning to Work With Spirit

Q: What did the spirit say to the ghost?
A :"Do you believe in people?"

Spirit does believe in us. In fact, most spirits that I have encountered believe in people more than most people do. Spirit likes to work with us. It comes bounding in like an enthusiastic puppy to assist and help us become fully empowered. Working with spirit is easy and safe. Like everything that we have discussed so far, there are rules. The rules for working with spirit are a little different from the things we have previously discussed in this book.

Spirit and Spirit Entities
There are many different types of spirit entities that wish to have direct communication with us if we learn how to listen. We will discuss the different types of entities a little further along.

All of these different aspects can co-operate together and really push a message at us for our own good. This is 'universal' or 'great' spirit, it has less personality and is often referred to as just "Spirit." It will try and give us universal messages to the questions we ask either verbally or with our life style, if we learn to listen to it. *Spirit speaks the universal language of symbols, sensations and emotions.* Pain and disappointment are the universal billboard signs to stop and not repeat things that are not working for us. Joy and prosperity is the thumbs up from spirit, letting us know that we have gotten it right.

You Can Learn To Communicate With Spirit
Though the style of message may vary the basic principles of working and communicating with any type of spirit are the same.

- Learning to communicate with spirit is a matter of paying attention.

With universal spirit you need to know the language of universal symbols. This is discussed further in my "Talking Tarot." With other spirit, you still have to know what you are looking for, as we have already discussed with Magellan's Ships, and you have to learn the simple steps. This book assists you through those steps so that you don't have to go through this learning curve alone.

I went through that learning curve alone and it was a frightening and lonely experience. In western culture our society is taught to ridicule or fear these abilities through the negative media images. People with these gifts are isolated and shunned. When my abilities began to make themselves felt, the people in my childhood congregation were terrified. Though I hadn't changed and was still a good girl, they claimed that I had become demonic and refused to talk to me. All except for one friend made me feel cursed. This friend, Lisa Thompson, told me that one day I would find away to use these abilities to help others and I have. By contrast, in traditional cultures these gifted children are spotted early and trained to become a valued member of their community.

Even though Alison Dubois, pictured here with Thomas Owen, and myself, in Fig 1, has always had a strong gift, she had to learn the rules of spirit communication too. We are not talking about a mere visualisation during a meditation; we are talking about calling in intelligent spirit entities that want to work along with you. Do not mix this up with the skills that you acquired for intention with Prana.

Fig 1 Shé with Alison Dubois and Thomas Owen

- Prana is not spirit. Prana is just a force that can nourish and strengthen.
- Spirit and spirit entities have intelligence and personality yet they have little or no intention nor desire to direct themselves. They are helpful and willing to work with you and your intentions.

The Two Main Rules Of Working With Spirit

1) If you call Spirit it comes

This is what is meant to "Invoke Spirit." Giving it "voice" (voke) from with-"in" ourselves.

Calling In Spirit
Here are two pictures of me calling in spirit to bless a couple that I am marrying. Firstly, I tie the hands to perform a handfasting, which is a traditional Irish wedding ceremony, and then I invoke spirit. These images capture on photographic film show how it came in as a rainbow to bless the couple. Photos of Reiki practitioners often show a form of rainbow spirit. It was far easier to capture spirit on film than with digital photography. Old photographic plates are far more effective, often revealing the faces of dead loved ones over the shoulders of the living.

2) If you ask Spirit to go it MUST leave

If spirit ever behaves in a troublesome, overly pushy or in a far too playful manner, you have every right to ask it to leave. The spiritual law is that it must leave if requested to do so. This is a natural law like gravity. It works! So just be strong, fearless and respectful but firm. Never order a spirit to do anything. Respectfully request its assistance and co-operation or departure. Manners, whether dealing with humans or spirit, always result in a greater amount of cooperation.

Fig. 2. The two progressive photos were taken by a professional photographer, Amanda James of Sydney, of Shé performing a handfasting ceremony, calling in the blessing of spirit upon the marriage of Susan and Shannon Lacey. Spirit is clearly seen coming in as a rainbow when called. This is a common phenomenon.

Always answer any questions asked of you by spirit candidly, honestly and fearlessly. If it should ask you why it should do as you ask, you must reply, *"Because I ask you and I am equal to you."* If the spirit ever becomes mischievous or tries to scare you, remain unmoved and tell it "... not to be so rude as you are not rude to it ..." Never show fear, as you have nothing to fear.

- Spirit cannot harm you.

People harm people or people harm themselves. Spirit cannot do anything to harm you. It is incorporeal. If you feel you may be afraid, do not begin this work. If you feel you are giving way to fear, laugh, even if it is fake, just laugh, as it will change the mood of the entity before you. They will laugh with you or it will embarrass them and they will leave out of embarrassment. When spirit tries to be mischievous or play tricks on you, it is usually a very comical situation as long as you are not looking through fear goggles. If you are afraid then spirit gets to laugh at you. If you are not afraid then you get to laugh at spirit behaving so ridiculously.

- So NEVER be afraid of working with spirit

Types of Spirits
You can learn to identify a variety of spirit beings. Most are helpful, but some are better at some jobs than others. Different types of spirits are appropriate to different things psychic tasks. To understand, ponder this example: If you were moving house, you would not ask your invalid grandmother to help you lift heavy boxes. However, if you needed advise from someone who had acquired a lot of life experience she would be the prefect person to help you. Similarly, if you were wishing to contact a departed spirit, you would not invoke a planetary entity. These spirit individuals, though helpful, are appropriate to different things. Lets perform a guided meditation that will put you in contact with Angels, Guides and Elementals and then let us examine some other forms of spirit entities and see what things they are best suited to help us with.

Opening the Crown Chakra
Your connection to the divine realm is established through your crown chakra so lets activate it first.
- Put your hands on your head and feel around

- Find the dent slightly forward of your crown that used to be your fontanel when you were a baby. The fontanel is the soft spot on a baby's head where the skull had not yet closed. This soft spot does not grow bone over it until a child reaches five years of age. Children are actively connected to spirit here and often sit chatting to fairies, spirit beings, and imaginary friends because of this strong connection.
- When you have located it, rub it using the tips of both index fingers.
- You will find yourself smiling as this is called "The Happy Spot" in acupuncture. If you continue rubbing it, you may find yourself giggling without good cause.
- Rub hard on this spot then push and slowly release.
- Close your eyes and focus on the spot.
- Visualise breathing in deeply and out slowly through this spot
- Take ten deep breaths this way
- Open your eyes
- What did you feel?
- Did you experience a tingling sensation at the crown chakra?

Did you experience a sensation of coolness?
- Coolness indicates a connection with the entities known as **Angels**. They are beings that have never been corporal and thus their energy is cool and quiet. They are very idealistic but can be a bit harsh and judgmental as they have little sympathy for the human condition because of their lack of experience with the physical realm.

Did you experience a sensation of Heat?
- Warmth indicates a connection to nature spirits or **The Fay Realm**, especially the elemental realm of our

warm earth. They can be playful tricksters with a great sense of humour or very nurturing and motherly. They enjoy life and are fun. They are intimately involved with manifesting the physical realm and matter.

Did you experience a sensation of height or your awareness expanding into the cosmos?
- A sense of getting larger or taller indicates a connection with your **Guides**. Guides are the higher or larger part of you. Sometimes called the Atman, the H.G.A. or Holy Guardian Angel. Albert Einstein called them his genius or genii, and said he felt that all inspiration comes through them. Though these can manifest as an aspect of you from another gender or another culture, i.e. North American Indian, Middle Eastern or Atlantean, they will take on whatever form you will pay the most attention to.

Your work with spirit is by no means limited to your first or strongest connection. You will eventually work with a group of spiritual friends that come from each of the varying spiritual categories. We have spoken about Angels, Guides and Elementals. Here are some others you will work with:

Spirits of Nature
These are the life force and intelligences of all natural things such as trees, rivers and land formations such as Ayers Rock or Mt Kaliash. These combine to produce a spirit of place, a unique character of each natural environment. It is common to physically see an elfish face in the bark of a tree, a rocky outcropping or a cloud formation. These are solidified manifestations of spirit, not as warm and malleable as the realm of flesh but

close to it. These nature entities will interact with you the more you try to become consciously aware of them. Meditating outdoors in these areas will encourage this interaction. You will begin to experience their personalities as Fairies, Divas or other creatures from mythology.

Spirits of Dead

Though most people in their lifetime will experience an encounter with a ghost, not everyone will be able to make conscious contact with people who have passed over into spirit. The people who can are called mediums. When the deceased wish to contact the living to provide closure it is always very emotional. As is evidenced by these endorsements:

> "Thank you for contacting my recently departed son for me. It gave great comfort to both me and (Name omitted as this is his young pregnant girlfriend) You're not like other mediums; you are very compassionate and cried as much as I did. You're very human and down to earth ... Thank you for your tenderness... There is no guessing and no apologies. Just direct thoughts, feelings and very straight answers, that we know must be his..." Mrs M Bundaberg
>
> ...thank you for contacting my daughter who had died... They erected a memorial for her and the others who were in the car accident in Townsville. It answered many questions left lingering about how the accident occurred.... It is good to know that she has moved on to her new life and whom she has been reincarnated as. Thank you ....for crying right along with me.... You are a special soul doing special work. - Mrs W Townsville
>
> "Shé you blew me away when you started laughing and joking around and acting just like my best friend did before he died in the car accident. You will be pleased to know we have held the funeral now just the way he described, through you, the way that he wanted it. It was so him...." Shelly, Dubbo NSW

People who only perform mediumship usually experience early burnout. Spirits of the recently deceased can pop their heads in when you are doing other psychic work.

You must be firm with them and do not let them be pushy. Their emotions come through quite clearly and you may see or hear something that they say. Often they just give impressions. What was important to them, often no longer has any meaning now that they are dead. Death does not make anybody smarter; so don't expect them to have miraculously become all-knowing or saintly. You can ask them questions they may or may not answer; they usually have some agenda of their own. Once they or their loved ones find closure the departed will move on and leave behind only an echo that can be read via psychometry. There are rules to medium work that are different from other esoteric work:
- The deceased can be pushy. Be firm. Insist on your own space and time. If they encroach, make an appointment with them on your own terms and in your own time, then they will wait to be heard.
- Because they were recently corporal, you will find that you become covered in an oily film of ectoplasm. It looks like your skin has become greasy. Shower when your sessions are finished and make sure that you wash this off before you go to bed otherwise you will remain open to spirits of the dead all night and you will wake up feeling hung over.

Spirits of Planets
Most of us are aware of the influence that the heavenly bodies can exert on our lives. The full moon affects the tides in our bodies. The ancients worked with seven heavenly bodies being the Sun, the Moon, Mercury,

Venus, Mars, Jupiter and Saturn. Hermetic practitioners worked with the spiritual intelligences of these spheres. These intelligences exert such a strong influence on our lives that the classical world considered them divine. When we need aid to change something significant in our lives, these spiritual beings can be called upon to give great aid and support. This is beyond astrology. It is good to become aware of the planetary cycles and what is happening in the heavens above you that can be affecting you, and making specific energies available for you to link into right now.

Spirits of Time
Time takes on a different meaning during spiritual work. Time does not move in a one directional line. Physics has accepted the curvature of space-time, which is part of the theory of relativity. Mystics have described time as a cycle, a curved ellipse for millennia. Sometimes this is depicted as an ouroboros; that is a snake eating its own tail. To spirit there really is no time, there is only an eternal moment of *now*.

Spirits from different time-periods can be called forward. Try this exercise:

The Clairvoyance Game
- Light a candle in a darkened room
- Do the Zigi meditation.
- Become the clear, calm pool of reflection.
- Look at the space just above the top of the flame of the candle.

- You will see a rainbow coloured aura there.
- Look through this to a mid point beyond.
- Breathe and find the clear, calm pool of reflection.
- The pool of reflection and the blackboard behind your eyes will appear with your eyes open.
- Stay focused on a point in space just above the top of the candle flame.
- Think of a departed friend, until you can actually see that friend's face quite clearly.
- It may take 10 minutes do this, but persist until you succeed.
- Now try a face from history.
- You will be able to practise clairvoyance in time as well as space, for there is no time and no space in spirit.
- Eventually you will be able to view scenes from history in that space just as you can look at a movie!

Totem Spirits

Totem or animal spirits are supportive. Your totem will eventually identify itself to you. It will be a special helper. If it is the reflection of a material earthly creature, like a hawk, not a mythical creature like a unicorn, and is sighted in the real world, you should pay special attention to it. If your totem is a mythical creature and you see a representation of it somewhere, pay attention and look for coincidences. Whether mythical or actual the sighting of your totem means they will have a non-verbal message for you. Try to understand. The more attention you pay to it the easier it will be to receive the message. To find your totem spirit animal perform this visualisation meditation.

Talking To The Animals Game
- Perform the Zigi meditation in a relaxed laying position
- Become the clear, calm pool of reflection.
- Go to your psychic workroom.
- Begin by visualising going on a long journey.
- The sensation of visualisation will vanish and you will find yourself travelling in a beautiful wild countryside in your mind.
- After journeying for what seems like a long time, you come upon a clearing and make a camp to rest.
- You take two portions of food from your pack, sit them in front of you, and wait.
- There will be a rustling in the bushes and your totem animal will appear.
- Do not be afraid if it is a large scary animal, nor disappointed if it is a small seemingly insignificant animal. They have a message for you, this is a part of who you are.
- This is your Daemon, or your long lost childhood soul. You welcome each other as long lost friends.
- Eat with your totem,
- Dance together.
- Then sleep.
- In your sleep it teaches you things that have escaped your notice.
- When you wake from your meditation write down what your totem animal was and any impressions or messages it left you with.

The Others
There are as many forms of spirit as there are species of life on this planets. Most spirits that do not fall into any

major category. I just call spirits of the spiritual realms or The Others.

Still when you work with spirit you don't want any rude intrusions from any unwanted or mischievous entity. You need to be able to focus without interruption and the best way to do this is to establish a protected sacred space to do your psychic work in. This is basic psychic hygiene. Here follows a time honoured method, called Circle Casting, for effectively sealing off an area psychically so that only the entities you want are called in and for dismissing all energies or entities that are called in when you have finished your work.

Calling In The "The Watchers" To Guard Over You
The Watchers or The Watchtowers are The Elementals, the spirits of Earth, Air, Fire and Water. They manifest to you in a form very appropriate to their element.
- *Gnomish creatures* that are wise, crafty, warm and dry are connected with the earth and can appear in your meditations on the earth element.
- *Sylphs* or airy-fairy creatures are connected to air and often physically manifest as a gentle breeze.
- *Salamanders* are what we call the fire elementals and they are warm, dry, passionate and manifest as a flame creature or a fiery lizard or bird in meditations.
- *Undines* are moist and very emotional, often seen as fluid, graceful merfolk in visualisations.

From the elements of earth, air, fire and water all matter emanates. They are intrinsically linked with guarding the realm of matter, and as such can be called upon to guard a sacred space for us in our work.

A good habit to get into is calling the four elements from the four directions before beginning any form of spiritual work.

Elemental Attributions

There are some very complex ways of calling the corners and deciding which of the elemental attributions you will give to which direction. The idea of calling the elements in particular directions comes from ancient Hermetic Magick. However, they invoked seven directions being: the four cardinal points, the universe above, the realm below and the point of the here and now on which you stand. As was common in Masonry, the Golden Dawn adopted only the four cardinal points, in their lower level initiatory workings, and reversed the compass point directions for two of the elements. Schools of Wicca adopted a simplified form of these directly from the Golden Dawn without the elemental or compass attributions reversed. These attributions were originally based on the position of the city of Alexandria in Egypt to the elemental forces around it.

The elemental attributions for the corner callings below are based on a general southern hemisphere east coast of Australia orientation. Elemental attributions can vary according to the position of the elements in the area. On the east coast of Australia, the Pacific Ocean, in which most of our water elementals dwell, is to the east. Therefore, in that area, the east is connected with the water element. In Western Australia, they are in the Indian Ocean, to the west. In the Northern Territory, they are in the North and, you guessed it, in South Australia, they are south in the Great Bight.

The orientation of the other directions should vary according to the elements around you. Generally in Australia, north is fire as it is hotter as we go north, and south is air, as it gets colder as we go south. The east coast will have the inland west as the earth element. However, on the west coast, inland is east. Therefore, in Western Australia the element of earth will be invoked from the east. These can also vary to localised conditions. For instance if you were in central Australia, surrounded by the earth elementals, where water is scarce and the main watering hole was north, you may feel that the water elements are speaking to you from that direction as this is the only source of water locally. You would then vary the other elemental associations according to the other local elemental associations. On a property surrounded by a triangle of rivers and dams you have a strong water element in every direction so being sensitive to the other elementals will determine your personal directional attributions.

Calling In The Elemental Guardians
Following is a basic corner calling that you can use. Alternatively, you can turn to the compass points and simply say "Spirits of earth, air, fire and water, please come here and watch over me whilst I do this spiritual work." That will work. However, the following is a more traditional method that works more effectively.

Always start in the east, as this is the direction that the sun rises. In the southern hemisphere, work *widdershins*, anti-clockwise to invoke and project energy out into the world, as this will raise a cone of energy. When you are finished, close, banish or dismiss *deosial* or clockwise as this forces a cone of energy down into the earth. This is the opposite in the northern hemisphere.1

East
Face east. You can perform a *Mudra* or hand gesture that amplifies what you are saying by raising your hands above your head to form a downward pointing triangle of manifestation for the water element with your hands. With thumbs touching and fingers pointing down. Alternatively,

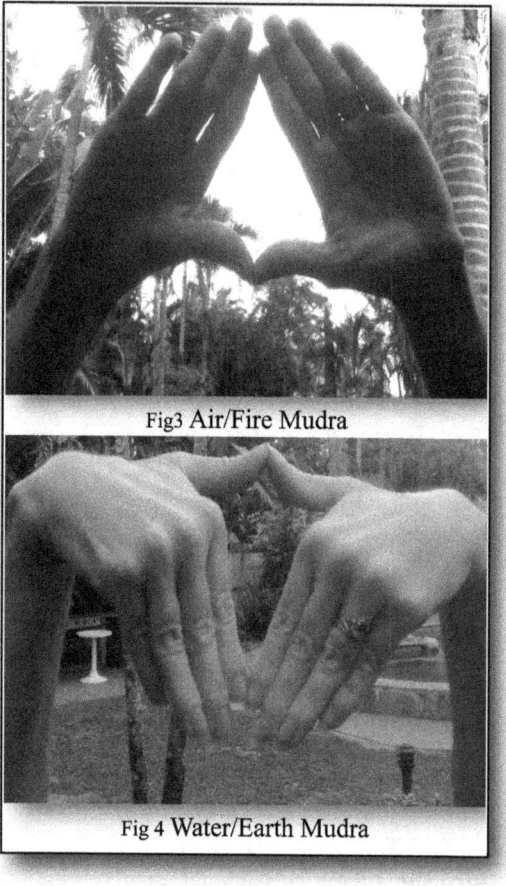

Fig3 Air/Fire Mudra

Fig 4 Water/Earth Mudra

have your palms up and facing to that direction. Then say:
"*Hail to the guardians of the watchtowers of the East.*
The elemental forces of water, love, emotion, life, light, fluidity, femininity, reincarnation, heaven, and Yin (You can add other attributions here if desired).
We stir, summon and call thee to be present with us and guard and watch over us.
Hail and Welcome!"

North

Face north. You can perform a mudra or hand gesture that amplifies what you are saying by raising your hands above your head to form an upward pointing triangle of manifestation for fire with your hands. With thumbs touching and fingers pointing up. Alternatively, have your palms up and facing to that direction. Then say:

"Hail to the guardians of the watchtowers of the North.
The elemental forces of fire, passion, energy, vitality, action, protection, masculinity, and Yang (You can add other attributions here if desired).
We stir, summon and call thee to be present with us and guard and watch over us
Hail and Welcome!"

West

Face west. You can perform a mudra or hand gesture that amplifies what you are saying by raising your hands above your head to form a downward pointing triangle of manifestation for earth with your hands. With thumbs touching and fingers pointing down. Alternatively, have your palms up and facing to that direction. Then say:

"Hail to the guardians of the watchtowers of the West.
The elemental forces of earth, nurturing, growth, strength, stability, mother, darkness, death, underworld and Yin (You can add other attributions here if desired).
We stir, summon and call thee to be present with us and guard and watch over us.
Hail and Welcome!"

South

Face south. You can perform a mudra or hand gesture that amplifies what you are saying by raising your hands above your head to form an upward pointing triangle of

manifestation for air with your hands. With thumbs touching and fingers pointing up. Alternatively, have your palms up and facing to that direction. Then say: -
"Hail to the guardians of the watchtowers of the South.
The elemental forces of air sleep, breath, power, speed, speech, ideas, intellect, Father and Yang (You can add other attributions here if desired).
We stir, summon and call thee to be present with us and guard and watch over us.
Hail and Welcome!"

Then walking widdershins, circling around your working area, say:
"Open now are the four gates
The fifth for spirit they create
Here is no future here is no past
Sacred within, the protective circle is cast."

Dismissing The Elements

After you have invited the elemental forces to attend and hold the position of spirit guardians of your sacred space, it is important to dismiss them and not leave them hanging. Begin your dismissal again in the east. Working *deosil* or clockwise through the cardinal points. Here follows a quick basic dismissal:

East

Raise your hands in the mudra for water above your head and in a clear strong voice recite: -
"Hail guardians of the watchtowers of the east.
We thank you for attending and safeguarding us.
Hail and Farewell!"
All repeat: *"Hail and Farewell!"*

South
Raise your hands above your head in the mudra for air and in a clear strong voice recite:
"Hail guardians of the watchtowers of the south.
We thank you for attending and safeguarding us.
Hail and Farewell!"
All repeat: *"Hail and Farewell!"*

West
Raise your hand above your head in the mudra for earth and in a clear strong voice recite:
"Hail guardians of the watchtowers of the West.
We thank you for attending and safeguarding us.
Hail and Farewell!"
All repeat: - *"Hail and Farewell!"*

North
Raise your hand above your head in the mudra for fire and in a clear strong voice recite: -
"Hail guardians of the watchtowers of the North.
We thank you for attending and safeguarding us.
Hail and Farewell!"
All repeat: *"Hail and Farewell!"*

Then walking deosil around the outside of your circle say:
"The sacred circle is open but unbroken. Merry Meet. Merry Part and Merry Meet again!"

Now that we have learnt how to create a protective sacred space in which to work, it's time to learn to apply our abilities! You are about to add the abilities to perform
- Psychometry
- Remote Viewing
- Medical Intuition

- Healing and Absent Healing to the abilities you have already learnt so far.

OK are you ready for this?

Practical Application of Psychic Abilities
For psychic abilities to have practical applications in your day-to-day life you will need to practise, especially for the following skills. You will be better at some of these skills than others. Make sure you practise the ones that you are not as good at more than the rest. To be successful in your psychic studies, you will need to use the three magical gifts we were all given at birth. They are fearlessness, tenderness and perseverance. Some people have rejected or forgotten these. Now is the time to remember these gifts.

Review points to remember to practise in conjunction with the new skills that follow next: -
- With all you do, breath deeply.
- Become the clear, calm pool of reflection.
- Allow yourself to feel your own immense power via The Zigi
- The point of power is in the present moment.
- The point of your own power is in your breath.
- Breath powered intent creates movement and manifestation.
- All illusion, separation and propaganda can be overcome by mastering the art of conscious breath

This photo was taken by Jenny Gersekowski
on the 20 of July 2008
of Shé giving a talk on "Spirit Communication,"
At The City Golf Club, Toowoomba Australia and a ghostly hand can be clearly seen in the foreground waving trying to get Shé's attention

Seven Psychic Secrets

Skill 4

Psychometry

Skill 4
Psychometry

Psychometry is: The ability to touch something and read the energy on it.

This can be used on a person, a photo or an object that once belonged to that person. Being able to touch something and feel what the person once felt, or is currently feeling is based on extreme empathy and tenderness. During psychometry, the illusionary barriers between the reader and the client come right down. The emotional glass wall that many naturally gifted individuals use as a protection shatters. The energies merge and become one. The reader steps into the client or object and can feel exactly what that person is feeling or has felt. Your heart begins to open to others and you will find yourself moved to action from extreme tenderness and empathy. You will feel the pain, humour and joy of others. You can use the energy bubble technique on page 80 to bubble yourself up and protect yourself when this becomes too much.

By being willing to assist others by opening yourself up to the tragedy of life, you will gain a sense of the cosmic comedy of existence. By deeply connecting and mirroring the world around you, you will become aware of the basic goodness that is everywhere in all things. Because of this basic goodness, you will begin to see everything on this planet as co-operating with you. The sensation is a state of vastness. You are moving towards living Zigi.

Opening The Heart Chakra

To develop psychic abilities only by developing the third eye or crown chakras will make us unbalanced. The legendary occultist Eliphas Levi claimed that opening the third eye without developing the heart chakra will lead to mental instability. Though this is not a hard and fast rule in every case, I have, as I am sure that you have, experienced my share of esoteric nutcases. Many suffer spiritual indigestion with all that stuff whizzing around in their heads but not the compassion to know what to do with it. The homeless people you see sitting on street corners muttering to themselves are very psychic. Their head is receiving several streams of information without the ability to sort it into what is emotionally essential. They become like a radio picking up several stations at once. Nothing is clear, the information is jumbled and garbled. Fine-tuning is needed. Compassion is the key to tuning in. Prana focused through the lens of the heart shows the way. The focused breath with intention forms a clear link. Deep compassion is essential for developing accurate psychic abilities.

- Emotion not information is the cornerstone of psychic craft.

It is essential to open the heart chakra before performing psychometry. This meditation will open your heart wide to others. With practice, as with the Zigi, the time taken and the number of conscious breaths with intent needed to get you into this zone will decrease.

- Place both of your hands palm down on your chest over your heart.
- Feel your heart beating with your hands.

- Lift your hands to approximately three to six centimetres, that is one or two inches, away from your chest.
- Perform the Zigi ten-breath meditation.
- Become the clear, calm pool of reflection.
- Breathe out of your hands and into your heart.
- Create a bubble of energy between your heart and your hands.
- Your hands will keep your heart safe.
- You will feel tingling warmth building in a reciprocal circle between them.
- Your heart will become more tender. It will fill and swell. If tears come to your eyes, this is OK. You are one with everything.

When finished performing psychometry remember to reverse this process and reduce the size of the heart chakra bubble. This will eventually happen automatically. However, once the heart chakra is opened psychically, you will remain more sensitive. In many spiritual cultures it is traditional to wear a scarf, pashmina or shawl across the back of the neck, as this helps protect the heart. The back of the neck is the main receptor site for the heart chakra.

Psychometry Game
Once your friends know that you are endeavouring to develop your psychic abilities you will have no end of volunteers all with their hands up for a reading. The humble barbecue will become a very busy time for you, as one by one people will ask you to read for them.
To practise psychometry with them:
- Ask them for a piece of personal paraphernalia like a ring or keys or glasses.

- If you and they feel comfortable, you can hold their hand
- Always ask permission before touching anyone even just on the hand. Apart from just being polite you should always ask, as some people do not like to be touched. It is an ethical consideration too. In today's litigious society touching someone without their express permission can be considered assault and you do not want to end up in court.
- Make sure that you practise both a) holding their hands and b) by just holding a personal item.
- Take ten Zigi breaths.
- Become the clear, calm pool of reflection.
- See the blank blackboard form behind your eyes.
- Allow any images to form there.
- Allow any sounds to come into the pool of reflection.
- Allow any smells to waft through your consciousness.
- Allow any tastes to tingle in your mouth.
- Allow any sensation to be felt in your body or emotions.
- All of these impressions are correct, none of them is wrong. Don't worry about any illusionary wrongness.
- Feed them back to your client.
- Allow the client to give them meaning.
- Ask them for their feedback on the things you have reflected to them so that your confidence in your own abilities will build.

You will amaze yourself at just how accurate you can be with this technique right from your very first attempt.

Delayed Verification

> Dear Shé, I am writing to you on behalf of my husband, Jason, whose reading you did at Hervey Bay recently.... I guess we had a delayed confirmation. (Whilst performing psychometry) ...you had told my husband how you saw his (deceased) Father working on something, like a pump. You also told him how Dad was concerned about dirty water getting near some feed, Lucerne or grass etc. You also told my husband how Dad kept mentioning someone named Ken and a business deal that he shouldn't do. Well, my husband had been mowing Dad's yard and during the day had been concerned about the amount of water coming out of the sullage hose. He tipped some grass clippings onto the area (instead of using them for feed, something he never does) and had a feeling to keep his feet out of the water. Lucky he did! Later that evening, all the power points wouldn't work in the house and the safety switch kept tripping out. We turned everything off, when my husband said he wondered if it was the sullage pump. It was! (Thank goodness he didn't step into the water on the grass clippings or he would have died.) So, my husband had to pull the pump out and the next morning arrange to get another. "Ken's Plumbing" was twice the price, so we did not buy it from there!
> So, we just wanted to let you know and thank you. Since then we have had many unexplained signs from Dad (now we know he is watching over us we pay attention to these) and my husband, Jason

You can reflect accurate information to your client and they will just look at you blankly. This is Ok. Leave it with them as bonus information that will make sense to them later. Why does this happen? Sometimes the process of the reading is a little overwhelming and they go blank and cannot connect up even the most glaringly obvious facts until they have relaxed and thought about it. Some time the facts reveal themselves later. This is a syndrome called delayed verification. As is shown by the following endorsement.

Sometimes people can go into a kind of shock when they receive personally meaningful information that shakes their belief system, as deep down they didn't believe in psychic abilities, and then bang, it hits them that there's no other explanation. They can be in such a turmoil they can't think straight.

Other times people just don't get the answer that they are hoping for and this can shock them as they were expecting something else and it takes time to change perspective. However, you can only tell the client what you see feel or pick up. It can be tempting to try and tell your client what they want to hear. Don't ever do this. It will backfire on you.

It is ultimately rewarding if you stick to giving your client only what you pick up. Be the psychic reporter not the psychic interpreter and it will work out as it should. As an example, I once had a gentleman come to see me, late in the evening, in distress about his estrangement from his mother. The only thing I could pick up with psychometry was a blue floral couch. He was very upset and left in a huff. About two hours later I received an apologetic phone call from him. He explained that what I had picked up had been 100% accurate and that it had helped heal the problem. He told how he had huffed away from our consultation and that he had huffed straight over to his mother's house, in an attempt to find an amicable solution for himself. When his mother opened the door to receive him he was able to see that behind her was a blue floral fold out couch she had purchased that day so that he could stay over and attempt to rectify their rift.

Another incidence of delayed verification happened to me in front of millions of viewers on *The One* when I had to do a reading on a piece of rock memorabilia, a wristband that had belonged to Freddie Mercury, the deceased former lead singer of UK super group Queen. I was

Seven Psychic Secrets

blindfolded and asked to identify as many personal points as possible about the original owner. The things I detailed were very personal; thought they were able to confirm several of the point that I had made, most were too personal and obscure for rock historians Glen A. Baker and Molly Meldrum to be able to confirm and they went a bit blank.

What the viewers were not able to see was that the delay for verification didn't take too long after that as the owner of the memorabilia, Gareth Hall, who confesses to being "considerably obsessed with the life and times of Freddie Mercury," and also plays the part of Freddie Mercury in The Australian Queen Tribute Show, stood up and confirmed my reading to be 100% accurate.

Gareth, in his press release, claims:
"I can personally verify that Shé's ability to gain information about the one-time owner of this wristband was nothing short of amazing! Almost all of her comments regarding Freddie Mercury were accurate as follows:
- *'This person put 110% into their performance'– That was certainly true of Freddie Mercury*
- *Shé kept complaining of sore and heavy legs and stated that she got a feeling of falling over. It is a little known fact that in the last few weeks of Freddie Mercury's life he had extremely weak legs. In the filming of his last ever video* (These Are The Days Of Our Lives) *it was reported by people close to Freddie that he kept falling backwards onto some cushions/pillows that had been set up for him as he was unable to stand for extended periods of time. He had also been suffering for a few years with a lesion on one of the*

soles of his feet, which caused him a great deal of pain right to the very end.
- *Shé commented that there was an 'unusual sharp angled room in this person's home'. It is also a little known fact that there was an octagonal shaped room in Freddie's house.*
- *Shé commented that she could hear many guitars around this person. This may seem obvious as the topic of the show was rock stars, however Queen's guitarist, Brian May, was very well known for creating harmonies with his guitar and then layering them to produce a large sound. The sound of guitar is definitely a very defining factor of Freddie's music.*
- *Shé mentioned that the name John was prominent. This is pertinent in that John Deacon was the Bass player for Queen. John was the last person to join the band and was probably the closest to Freddie. Freddie took John under his wing and protected him in many ways, especially in the early years. John has totally withdrawn from the limelight since Freddie's death.*
- *Shé mentioned the King Tarot card in her reading. This amazed me due to the obvious regal/royal link. In addition, Freddie Mercury would often finish his show with a King's Crown on his head ..."*

Freddie Mercury, The King, With a Sweatband

Gareth concludes by saying: *"I truly feel that Shé's reading of Freddie Mercury's wristband was extremely accurate. I also feel that ... many of the things she picked up on were indeed far more accurate than she was given credit for."*

Seeing Freddy From My Side
The energy I read from the memorabilia was, firstly, the intense pain and suffering of his final year and secondly, the impression of a deeply caring and private person so very different from his public persona. I believe the purpose of the reading was not for verification by the rock experts; rather the purpose was to bring healing to John Deacon who was most badly affected by the death of his close friend and mentor. Freddie's picking a national, top rating, psychic T.V show to platform this, demonstrates his flair for showmanship beyond the end. You will produce this level of result and better using the psychometry techniques in this chapter.

Skill 5
Remote Viewing

Skill 5
Remote Viewing

In simple terms remote viewing is: The ability to read energy when not touching something even if it is a long way from you.

Remote Viewing is a term developed as part of the U.S. military's research, development and application of psychic capabilities for gathering military intelligence. Every nation has a psychic unit in its intelligence agencies. Uri Gellar has been employed to identify targets for Mossad. The Former USSR and the UK openly admit to running such agencies. The most famous is "Project Stargate," the acknowledged U.S. military psychic spying project run by F. Holmes "Skip" Atwater using technology developed by Robert Monroe to train and control professional remote viewers, including the renowned Joseph McMoneagle. During the cold-war era. Those with natural psychic aptitude were used as U.S. Army counter-intelligence special agents.

Shé with Skip Atwater former head of the U.S. military psychic spying unit know as "Project Stargate." He is the skipper character portrayed in the movie/book "Men Who Stare At Goats"

Remote Viewing Is The Most Lucrative Psychic Skill

There are many remote viewers being paid very well to apply their professional skills to corporate applications. Corporate psychics are useful in business applications such as:

Building
Research and development
Security
Investment and share markets
Personnel
Publishing
Racing industry
Farming
Real estate
Fund raising
Indigenous liaison
Business Directions
Business Decisions
Personnel & Team Dynamics
Mining
Weather
Environment and location
Locating Resources
Outsourcing
Investments
Potential Issues
Conflict and Continuity

You can utilise intuition as an essential business tool to:
* Look ahead and see the outcomes of your business decisions: Working backwards from there is efficient.
* Looking ahead to see the outcomes of your business decisions, enables you to be able to workout the steps

you need to take, backwards from the future, to establish the necessary actions required today.
* Make better decisions
* Help you adapt quickly in a radically changing economic climate.

The application of intuition in business is brilliant for assisting with problem avoidance.

Having intuitive employees allows you to problem solve BEFORE the problems occur

I have been able to utilise this in my own successful businesses, which lead to me becoming a former Queensland Business Woman of the Year and being the founding editor of a successful alternative magazine.

An example of how lucrative remote viewing can be in business is a situation were a very large Melbourne firm, owned by a Melbourne base billionaire, once paid me $2000, plus I received a bottle of tequila, chocolates and flowers as a thank you gift, for ten minutes' work. $2000 represented 1% of the amount I saved them with the information. I supplied them the needed information via a single remote viewing session.

They asked me to locate micro fibres of a specific density and a specific length for below a specified price. These were needed for a research and development project. They could get the product from London or Singapore; however, shipping delays and costs would have increased the projected cost by a further $200,000

I received their call in between appointments. I didn't promise anything but I said I would see what I could do. My next appointment was ten minutes away. So I quickly focused for a minute till I became that clear, calm pool of reflection. In that state I received an image of a logo of a cement company. I looked up their number and telephoned their head office.

Their supply officer did not think I was crazy for asking a cement company about micro fibres. They were amazed as they had a load sitting forgotten in a shipping container in Sydney for which they were being charged storage fees.

They were happy to get rid of them at any price. I never went to the container yard. I did all this remotely from my office on the Gold Coast. I cannot reveal the name of either company as ethics prevents me.

Remote Viewing and Ethics
Maintaining high ethics is important to corporate clients. Never compromise your confidentiality and always maintain a reputation for ethics and they will trust you, and other companies will feel happy to work with you.

It is also important to insist on maintaining honesty even if it comes across as somewhat naive. Doing this resulted in my almost completely being cut from the Ned Kelly episode on the TV show The One.

On camera I said that I was clearly receiving that he was not buried where the contestants were asked to look for his remains. This was not what they wanted to hear. After giving the exact location of a dig site where other bodies were located, being 18 paces diagonally north east of the

X-marked centre tower, I insisted that the remains of Ned Kelly had been reclaimed decades before by his surviving family members in rural Victoria. Not what they wanted for the TV show. This may have been silly of me but it was honest. Now however I have been vindicated.

Mr Baxter, who has had guardianship of the Ned's skull, has finally come forward confirming this story. Living members of the Kelly family have offered genetic sampling to validate the claim so that they can reclaim the skull and give the body a proper burial. Though it disappointed the TV show it has resulted in lots more remote viewing clients that vale honesty and integrity[1]

Remote viewing can be used to: -
- Describe a distant or remote location or event.
- Gather hidden or concealed information or descriptions in the same room or remotely.
- Predict the choice of a variable target, meaning that the targets are determined after the remote-viewing sessions are completed.
- Be sensitive enough to reveal aspects of minute change in the same room or remotely.
- Predict from situations of multiple possible futures which future is the most probable and how to navigate to the one that will be the most profitable.

Our society is currently moving along the pathway to the acceptance of psychic abilities in the business place. In fact, this was the theme of the 27th annual meeting of the Society for Scientific Exploration. However, some farsighted individuals have always recognised the advantages of these abilities as did William Blake:

"To see the world in a grain of sand, and heaven in a wild flower, to hold infinity in the palm of your hand, and eternity in an hour."

Remote Viewing Game
- For this exercise, you will need to work with a friend.
- Each of you will need to draw a simple shape without letting your partner see.
- Fold it over and put it in to an envelope.
- Swap envelopes by placing it on the table in front of your working partner.
- Do not touch the envelope that you are reading.
- Do the Zigi Meditation.
- Become the clear, calm pool of reflection
- See the blank screen form behind your eyes.
- Allow any images to form there.
- You will receive components of the image in flashes.
- Draw down on your own notepad whatever components you see.
- Do not try to interpret what the whole image is.
- Do not guess and try to form it into a picture that makes sense.
- Just draw down a corner or a curved line etc. in the order that you see them.
- When you have received enough images, usually 15 minutes is sufficient, open the envelope and see how you have done.
- You will be impressed with yourself. If not, practise it again. Remote viewing is easy and it does not take long to become quite good at it.

You can also use *The Clairvoyance Game* to do remote viewing.

Skill 6
Medical Intuition

Skill 6
Medical Intuition

Medical Intuition is: The ability to use Remote Viewing or Psychometry to read the energy inside a person.

The purpose of all psychic abilities is healing. There is a right way to go about medical intuition. A way that protects you and your client. There is no point draining or hurting yourself to help another. The goal is for there to be one less person in pain in the world, not to just swap one for another.

The feeling of medical intuition is like stepping inside your client's body. You feel what they feel. You will experience their pain. If the pain grows too strong step back, withdraw your awareness to your own body, and put a protective bubble around yourself.

I had a client called Tom come to me. He initially refused to tell me his problem. He wanted to test me out. Test worked! I very accurately pinpointed his stomach cancer. Because of my psychometric talent and my deep empathy I picked up his stomach pain so strongly it made me fall off the couch, rolling on the floor holding my stomach. He was on painkillers - I was not. He did not warn me it was serious, but he should have. I recovered enough to give him a healing section and he performed some daily exercises I gave him. Not only did his cancer go into remission but some interesting side effects occurred which he attributed to the spiritual therapy. He also suffered from a profound hearing problem and it improved, as did his relationship with his father. He also regained the desire to live. I told him that "*Things would shift on many levels for him,"* and they certainly did. Most importantly his life became what he wanted it to be.

Healing is the goal of all psychic abilities. Psychic abilities are triggered by the need to assist others. Assist them to do what?
- To heal, mentally and physically,
- To overcome life's problems and
- To make things better for others and hopefully yourselves too.

Non-Competitiveness
It was hard for the producers of *The One* to understand that. There was no competition between us even though they had advertised the show as a quest to find Australia's best psychic. It was really who was the most popular not the most skilled psychic. All the way through the show we were all assisting each other to succeed.

This was most evident with Amanda, the only non-professional psychic among us. When we first met her she was young and inexperienced but had loads of enthusiasm, natural talent and no trained skills. We were all a bit surprised that someone who describes herself as "just a tree hugging hippy" was among us. With each task we all took her aside and gave her advice. She had the six best psychic teachers in Australia, so she was bound to advance quickly. She made very rapid progress. We became more proud of her each time she succeeded. It felt like our little girl had done so well! She had to end up as one of the top three. You will do very well too!

Changing Fate

People are not fated to be ill nor to die. People are borne disabled because of some human reason, not because of fate. A trained and fully empowered psychic's mission is to aid others to be all that they can be. The client's life should improve after seeing a skilled psychic. The skilled psychic reader looks at the personal life map laid before their client and can tell them what points of interest they will encounter next, what is in store for them, where they have been, and ultimately, if they stay on this chosen path where they will arrive. Yet, a good psychic never makes his or her client feel fatalised. Individuals choose their own course. Even if we make all the wrong decisions we can still change our fate right up until the last moment before an incident.

There are hundreds of accounts where people have changed their fate. These people have taken the warnings and advise and turned left instead of right and saved their own or someone else's life. The Nicholas Cage movie *Next* gives one of the best explanations of this phenomenon. A skilled psychic can help steer their client away from the warnings and towards the best choices for their future so that they become the master of their own destiny.

Client Confidentiality and Psychic Ethics
The ethics that a professional psychic must follow are similar to those practised by medical practitioner, often with more empathy. In order for a psychic to be effective they must be able to be trusted. They will gain a good reputation if they maintain high ethics.
- Client confidentiality.
- Refusal to look into a third party's business.

- Refusal to interfere in another's decision-making process, or
- Refusal to encroach on another's free will.
- Do no harm.

The above ethics are imperative. Gaining a position of trust is hared earned, once lost it can never be restored. Therefore, this profession needs to maintain the moral high ground. 'Unfortunately there are some charlatans, unethical psychics and frauds out to make money by preying on people's vulnerabilities. Their bad reputation can drag us all down and the result could be cataclysmic. If you are in doubt please contact your county's Psychic Association who will be able to recommend reputable practitioners.

Plato's warning - The Moral of Atlantis
One of the earliest tales of the consequences of a gifted society that removes its social constructs is Plato's written around 430B.C.E. tale of Atlantis, in his works "Timaeus" and "Critias." It is the tale of the advanced psychic civilisation that abandoned its ethics and values, Attempting to conquer ancient Athens, resulting in its destroying itself via a natural cataclysm. The theme of this story is repeated in each culture in many different forms. It is a fable warning about the consequences of not having clearly defined ethics. Yes, ethics can change but this legend warns that abandoning them all together results in a society not knowing who it is, and destroying itself.

Paratge (pronounced peerage) is an old Pagan concept of honour, nobility, freedom and responsibility, that includes a sense of balance with nature and the karma of The Threefold Law of return, empathy, courtesy, chivalry, gentility, high ideals, promoting a spirit of equality based on common virtue and deprecating discrimination based on blood, race, gender, sexual orientation, religion or wealth. This is an excellent philosophy for an empowered psychic to live their life by. As the troubadour practitioners of paratge were responsible for a great flowering of creativity in the 12th to 14th centuries so have the psychics been today

Living With Nobility, Freedom and Responsibility
Psychics, like any other specialised professional, deserve fair remuneration for their time. They have specialist skills that are valuable. The financially disadvantaged psychic can't help anyone, not even themselves. Fiscal reward gives you protection and freedom. The more freedom you have the more you can help others. There is no nobility in poverty. People who give their skills away usually end up making others feel obligated. This can be very manipulative. It is an inverted control and ego game. Beware the free readings; they often cost you far more in other ways. To truly live within the ethic of honour, nobility, freedom and responsibility, you need to go beyond ego and the internal dialogue. Make a decision to relinquish three things: -
1. The need to control.
2. The need to be approved, and
3. The need to judge.

These are the three things the ego is trying to do all the time. It is important to be aware of them every time they come up. Slipping away from ideals of nobility results from hanging onto any of these three things. Remember that *a great psychic has a diminished ego.*

Intimacy and Tact

Medical intuition is one of the most intimate things a person can do with another being. It is more intimate than sex. You can feel what another person is feeling inside and out. You can end up knowing more about a person than they do themselves and they will reveal things to you that they have never told another living soul. It is always best to read for a person when they are by his or herself. If they insist on a partner being there, be very diplomatic. Always be tactful when you express what you are reflecting. Skeptics often accuse tactful psychics of being obtuse. Legally and morally we have to be. Legally we are not allowed to scare, threaten or intimidate our clients. We are not allowed to tell someone if we see death and must wait until they express knowledge of a health concern before we can legally discuss it with them.

If your client has a delicate personal problem tell them in such a way that they end up actually saying it for themselves. They can accept it better that way. For instance you might say "I experience an irritation around the genital area for you." "Oh yes," the person may reply, "I have had a problem with herpes for a few years now." Let them tell you, it is far less embarrassing for them that way. On The One I did a reading for a man with prostate issues. I asked his permission before I announce this on national T.V in front of 1,500,000 viewers.

Always, always be as tactful as possible.

Medical Intuition Game

- You will need a willing volunteer for this reading, preferably one whom you know very little about.

- Never touch a client without their expressed permission.
- Ask your client if it is OK to touch them. The impressions are stronger this way but you can do this remotely too.
- Holding the hand should be sufficient but you can place your hand on the back of their neck if they feel comfortable.
- Do the Zigi ten-breath meditation.
- Feel any discomfort that you are experiencing yourself. Acknowledge it and put your own stuff to one side.
- Become the clear, calm pool of reflection
- Scan with your awareness from the top of your client's head right to the soles of their feet. Do not stop at the base chakra. Scan all the way down their legs and feet. Look for everything. Remember, if they have an ingrown toenail their lives will be miserable so don't miss it out.
- Whilst scanning you will feel the sensations inside your own body.
- Mention each sensation as it occurs.
- Describe what you are experiencing as best you can to your client. Unless you are a medical practitioner no one will expect you to do this in medical terms.
- Emotional sensations often come through with the physical sensations. If these arise mention these too. Mental and emotional distress are just as painful as physical distress. The two can often be linked.
- Allow your client to give feedback on each thing you mention to them as you progress.

This Medical Intuition Exercise is a good way to zone in on the energy of the individual at the start of a reading.

If you are picking up something that is obviously not theirs ask about their family and friends. They can be taking on and reflecting other people's stuff. It is surprisingly easy to read friends and family through your client by shifting the focus of your intent.

This exercise establishes the empathy link to your client. Remember to protect yourself with the energy bubble if you link in with pain as the endorsement below shows

> Dear She`
> Thank you for your assistance. I came to you without telling you my problem. I wanted to test you out. Test worked! You very accurately pinpointed my stomach cancer. I apologize for this because of your medical intuitive talent you picked up on my stomach pain so strongly it made you ill. I was on painkillers you were not. I did not warn you it was serious I should have. - I wanted to let you know that I have been performing the exercises you gave me daily. Now not only has my cancer gone into remission but some interesting side effects have occurred I believe as a result of the therapy. As you know I suffer from a profound hearing problem this has improved - as has my relationship with my father. As you said: `Things would shift on many levels for me` and they have. I have some friends who would like to come and see you. They want to know what has helped me so much. - I now want to live again. My life is becoming what I want it to be. Thank you I hope all goes well for you in everything you try to do. You deserve it.
> Tom

The next chapters show what your prana charged positive intentions can do to assist your client.

Skill 7
Healing and Remote Healing

Skill 7
Healing and Remote Healing

Healing and remote healing are: The ability to send energy to assist the healing process for illnesses intuitively diagnosed by you; whether or not you are touching the client, in the same room, area or country i.e. 'remotely.'

Once you have diagnosed your client with medical intuition, it is surprisingly easy for you to extend that knowing into an active healing. It is a natural extension of the function of the naturally helpful psychic. You just bubble up energy and consciously intend that it go to the affected area to treat the soul to heal the body, restore their being to a sense of wholeness by breaking the repeating patterns in their lives. How do you do this? You just have to charge up and intend to send the vital life force otherwise know as pranic healing energy to the right place and intend that it be so.

The natural state of the body is to heal itself. Any healer in any healing modality, allopathic or alternative, only assists the individual's natural healing process. This only ceases when there is something drastically wrong. Spiritual healing is the easiest way to treat an illness. Psychic healing does not just work on one level. It affects the whole being. Remember that, as mentioned in the section on The Chakras, we have physical, mental, emotional and spiritual bodies. If we can produce a shift in one the others must move too. If you shift some energy spiritually then you are giving your client a kick-start to health in all of their other bodies as well.

If you have skills as a medical doctor, psychologist, natural therapist, massage therapist, herbalist, counsellor, shaman, witch or any other skills you can use this to augment your psychic healing energy. You can affect these other bodies to produce a spiritual change as well.

None of this can replace commonsense. If you come in out of the rain, stay out of the midday sun and don't step on land mines you will, of course, be much better off.

As with the medical profession, so too with spiritual healing, "Do no harm" must be the first rule. Beyond that do the commonsense things as well. For example if they are physically ill and if they have not seen a General Practitioner encourage them to do so. Also work along with other healing modalities, doctor, chiropractor, naturopath, massage where appropriate.

By reflecting their own spiritual condition back to your client they can come to understand how and why they have manifested this illness or emotional addiction in their life. They begin to know that they have the power to overcome it if they choose to do so. Using these methods, many have reported relief from supposedly "incurable" and permanent illnesses from psychic healing.

You will find that you will be reflecting a lot of emotional discomfort back to your clients. You will help them to release the past hurts that sabotage them. They can come to understand that because they were hurt in the past they do not have to keep hurting themselves now. Then as the wheels of their life turn they begin to take your client into the direction they want to go. Your client can look at the future they are creating for themselves and see how to steer towards whole, healed, and successful the future they want.

Relationships, abuse, post traumatic stress disorder, and grief are common issues assisted by spiritual healing. This also helps your client heal the rifts they have in their relationships with:
- Their partner.
- Their children.
- Their parents.
- Their friends.
- Their colleagues.

Helping ease one individual's pain eases the pain on us all. Spiritual healing helps your client identify and move towards the spaces of commonality and compromise as they begin to realise that we are all one. These endorsements illustrate these points:

> Hello Shé
> I have been meaning to contact you for some time now; it has been ages since I last saw you in Melbourne... In my case I am healing very well and I am free of all my cancer and in a good headspace on a personal and business front. ...If you are in Melbourne in the coming months my shout for lunch, it would be great to see you, I promise I will try not to sponge too much of your great energy.
> Garry Crole
>
> Hi Shé
> I just wanted to update you (on my diabetes)... My energy level is better and I'm losing some weight. Thank you once again for your advice, I'll let you know how my sugar level is going in about a month, for now its ok.
> Take care, Regards Liz

Taking the Faith Out of Healing

Much scientific testing has been conducted on psychic especially for their healing talents. Again and again this has been proven via objective results not subjective feelings.

Many of these studies have been prompted by the astounding results achieved in the 1970s on Matthew Manning by Nobel Prize-Winning physicist Professor Brian Josephson. After which Josephson exclaimed:
"I think we are on the verge of discoveries that may be extremely important for physics. We are dealing with a new kind of energy. This force must be subject to laws. I believe that ordinary scientific investigation will tell us a lot about psychic phenomena. They are mysterious but no more mysterious than a lot of things in physics already. In times past respectable scientists would have nothing to do with it. Many of them still won't. I think that respectable scientists will find that they have missed the boat."[1]

In 1974 Mr Manning went on to be tested A New Horizons Research foundation in Toronto Canada by Dr. Joel Whitton in which he was shown to display a kind of brain wave pattern never reported previously from a part of the brain considered to be dormant.

In 1977 Mr. Manning allowed himself to be subjected to testing by The Mind Science Foundation San Antonio Texas, The University of California and London University This large number of tests demonstrated under laboratory conditions his ability to slow the rate of degradation of human blood cells and enzymes, hinder the growth rate of mould samples, remotely influence another persons brainwaves and accelerate the growth rate of rye grass seeds. About this Dr Jeffery Mislove said:

> "Our month long experience has yielded sufficient evidence to refute the arguments of those who maintain that this is fraud."[1]

Mr Manning could also accelerate the death rate of cancer cells. Dr John Kmertz comments on this:

> "The cancer cells were actually being killed by Matthew. In at least 60% of the cases the results were quite significant. When an individual who was not a healer tried the same thing nothing happened."

Mr Manning has lectured to the Oncology Section of The Royal Society of Medicine. Dr. Brian Roet, formerly of the Charring Cross Hospital, London, followed psychic healing closely after this and made the following comment:

> "I have seen many patients who have previously attended...healing; everyone of them, without exception, has gained considerably... My many years training as a doctor and an anaesthetist have taught me how much we do not know about the body and its healing processes. (Psychic healing) is not discussed in medical text books but I can verify their efficacy...from patients I have met."[1]

These were ground breaking studies, but studies that were performed on only one man. There continues to be true scientific testing of these abilities, too many to mention in this brief text, to this day with astounding results. So the evidence is there. True scientific studies have been done on many other people too in the ensuing decades with affirmative results since the mid 1970s. Those who claim that psychic healing does not work need to do their own research better!

The Healing and Remote Healing Game
This follows on naturally from medical intuition. So perform all the stages of the medical intuition game.
- Stand behind your client who is sitting in a chair.
- Perform the energy bubble game but push the energy bubble into their shoulder or back of neck to give them a kick start
- If the client feels comfortable push the energy bubble directly into the affected area.
- Your hands may heat up. If your client complains that your hands are getting too hot move your hands slightly away from the affected area. If you feel the need to move your hands around then tell you client clearly what you are doing. You will know when the healing session is finished because your hands will cool down.

IMPORTANT: Never touch socially unacceptable areas of your client's body. Not even if they give you permission to do so. This is illegal and unethical. Do not touch them in a compromising way even if they ask you too; you could end up in jail. Your purpose is to assist people, not take advantage of their vulnerability. Remember that you are in a position of trust and will be judged harshly if you abuse this. Always ask your client for permission to touch them before you touch them anywhere even on the hand.

Remote Healing

With remote healing the steps are exactly the same but the client is not in the room. It does not matter where in the world they are. There is neither time nor space in spirit. Bubble up the energy and send it, just like you threw it to your friend in the energy bubble game, and your clear intention will take it to the right person no matter where in the world they are.

Soul Retrieval

All healing begins by healing the psyche. Sometimes it may feel as though peaces of the person's soul or psyche are missing. Soul retrieval and rescue is the psychic healer's main job. In one form or another all healing is soul-retrieval. This method works well with depressed, grieving or emotionally scarred individuals but can also have profound physical effects too. An allegory is best used to describe the process. If you imagine most damaged people as wolves who have been caught in a trap and chewed off a paw in order to be able to survive a traumatic experience then it's easier to understand what a psychic healer will be doing during a soul retrieval session. People tear away pieces of their soul and psyche during trauma. The psychic healer's job is to find the lost piece and bring it back to them. The psychic then returns the energy of this lost piece back into the person's body symbolised by blowing.

This is a guided meditation for your client. Take your time do this slowly. Make sure that you stay with them and do not rush the words ahead of their ability to visualise.

- To begin a soul-retrieval session drum a slow and rhythmic beat or play some slowly rhythmic music.

- Get your client to lie down on their side comfortably or sit sideways in a chair.
- Have them breathe slowly and deeply from the top to the bottom of the lungs without holding their breath as with the ten prana breaths exercise.
- After about ten minutes say words to the effect of the following to your client:

A long time ago, you were knocked to the ground and were made to feel that you are not worthy. This is not true. You are (Name their Name)! In all that, that means. Yours is a special and difficult calling to most but for you it will be easy.

To become you, you have been through much. You have crossed the abyss and left a piece of your soul on the other side. However, you need all of your soul with you if you are to do what you must. Take back your soul and keep it safe, it is precious. If you are willing, I will help you make sure you have found it and retrieved it. Regaining all of your soul is your way to be worthy, worthy of being N/N.

- Then you will begin to take them on a guided meditation as follows:

We are going on a long journey. Close your eyes and we will journey in our mind together. From where you are now we will return to the edge of the abyss, through a parched and arid land. You faced the abyss once before and the event was so traumatic it changed you forever. You survived but in order to survive you left a piece of yourself behind. It left you wounded, a little less than you were but stronger than before more knowing more cautious. Yet this time I am with you. Now you are a seasoned warrior accompanied by their shaman in quest of the prize that will restore your lost kingdom to you its rightful owner. We will win. We will go beyond the abyss. You will be safe and we will find what you have left behind and restore it to you. I will guide you to it so that you can be reunited with your won power. Your kingdom will again be as great as anybody else's. No one will have power over you. You will rule yourself again. You will not be harmed. You will be whole healed and well.

We can see the chasm of the abyss way in the distance. As we get closer we see a narrow rope bridge across a great chasm. On the other side is the largest and most beautiful tree that you have ever seen. It contrasts the landscape. It has seven layers of branches. You can see three descending levels of branching roots under the ground, there is the immense heavy branches that bend under their own weight and touch the ground where you stand and three levels ascending into the heavens. The top most branches are so high they see to enter space. It is somewhere here, in this magnificent sentinel that the lost piece of your soul hangs, safely guarded, awaiting your return.

- Pause and allow time for them to absorb it all.

We have now reached the edge of the abyss and we must cross the bridge together. You may not want to go back there but we are completely safe and I am with you. If you see or feel anything tell me immediately what you experience.

- Wait for any feedback they give you.

The rope bridge sways but we step in unison. You must go first but I am right behind you. Keep your eyes on the tree and see how beautiful it is. Suddenly we are there. The rope bridge is way behind us. We are looking up and up and up at the branches of the tree. There! We can see the lost piece of your soul. Can you tell me what it is?

- Whatever the client tells you relate it to a chakra area. i.e. Legs relate to base chakra and settling down issues; Arms relate to giving, heart and love issues; Eyes relate to third eye and unwillingness to see. Let your intuition guide you.

Now we must climb the tree and get that piece back. The animals and birds in the tree are friendly and will help us. What level of the tree is it on?

- Again relate the client feedback to levels in the seven-chakra system. Roots can be the base chakra, the sexual chakra are the seeds growing deep within the tree, solar plexus is mid trunk, arms branching out from the heart chakra, throat is the upper mid branches, and the third eye and crown in the high branches etc.

We are climbing higher and higher but suddenly here it is. We are reaching out for it gently and tenderly, slowly as though it was a frightened bird sitting on the branch. Almost… There! We have it! We have it back! We pull it in towards us cradling it gently. Soothing it. Infusing it with life. I turn to you smiling. Are you ready to be reunited with the lost part of you? It is not in pain anymore and you will look after it much better not so that it does ever need to be left behind again. Hold still whilst I put it back into your body.

- Visualise restoring their being to a sense of wholeness. Picture the frayed nerve endings coming together and see in your mind's eye the piece/s they have described rejoin with the whole. Blow hot air strongly from your mouth through a funnel made from your hand, into the back of the chakra area indicated by the piece/s and branches that the client described.

A cloud has engulfed us in this high troc and we feel like we are floating. A hand is lifting us, carrying us back to a safe place. You can relax. The more you float the stronger you become till at last you feel as strong as before. Stronger. Invincible.

The cloud begins to dissipate, revealing that it has flown us home. You have returned, bringing that feeling of strength with you. When you are ready return your consciousness to the room and open your eyes.

- Allow your client to give you feedback.
- Soul retrieval complete.

Traditional Spiritual Healing Methods
You may wish to augment healing, remote healing and soul-retrieval and with these traditional methods for physical conditions.

Obligatory Disclaimer: The following traditional Tibetan Shamanic methods for treating physical conditions are given for educational purposes. No medical recommendation is inferred or suggested by any of the treatment methods outlined in this book.

- **Impaired Hearing**
- Breath into the ears warming them.

- Charge up the hands with an energy ball.
- Cup your hands over the clients ears to make a suction cup.
- Move the hands in and out to create suction down deep into the ear canal.
- Have the client cup their hands over their own ears to make a suction cup.
- Have the client move their hands in and out to create suction down deep into the ear canal.
- This should be repeated several times a day.
- Also use tapping method below on C4 and C7 vertebrae.

- **Memory Loss**
- Try to think of the thing forgotten.
- Stand and hold the head backwards with the eyes closed.

- **Headache**
- Charge up the hands with an energy ball.
- Then place them on the temples.

- **Digestive Problems**
  - Also upset tummy, morning sickness, slimming, and blood sugar levels.
  - Charge up the hands with an energy ball,
  - Tap firmly so as to produce a drumming sound about every three seconds on the C7 and T6 vertebrae with the index finger for approximately 1 minute.

- **Arrhythmia and Tachycardia**
  - Similarly tap on the 2nd and 4th thoracic vertebrae.
  - Teaching your clients prana breathing and heart chakra stimulation, can aid many heart ailments.

- **Bowl Movements**
  - Similarly tapping on 5th thoracic vertebrae.

- **Childhood Behavioural Problems**
  - Charge up the hands with an energy ball.
  - Similarly tap eight times only on the child's temples whilst making positive behavioural statements like "You are a

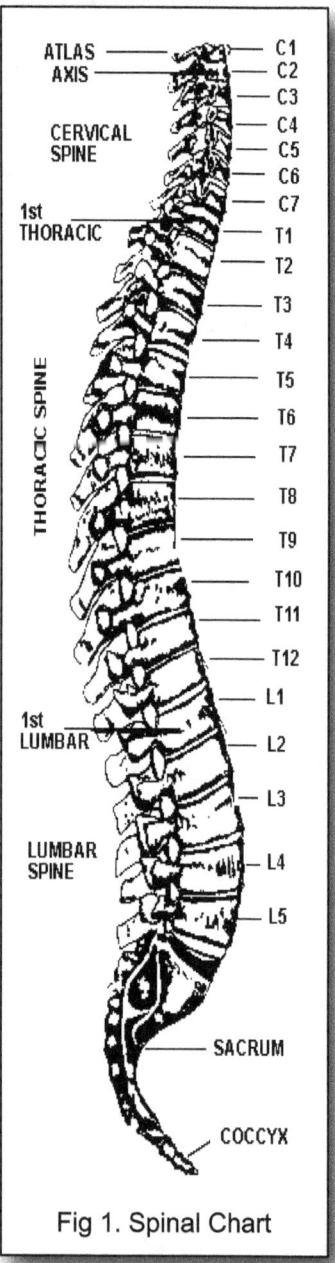

Fig 1. Spinal Chart

good boy." "You're very helpful." You are very creative."
- This aids these messages to anchor into the child's deep subconscious and begin to replace negative patterns.

- **Epilepsy and Motion Sickness**
  - Get the client to do the Zigi meditation to change their brain wave state.
  - Charge up the hands with an energy ball.
  - Place the hands on the head and the solar plexus and visualise gaping raw nerve endings coming together and healing.

- **Head Cold Congestion**
  - Charge up the hands with an energy ball.
  - Move the skin on the bridge of the nose up and down.
  - Have the client visualise being very strong and joyful whilst you are performing this for them.

- **Asthma**
  - Charge up the hands with an energy ball.
  - Close the nostrils alternatively and get the client to take a deep prana breath through each nostril.
  - Have the client visualise being very strong and joyful whilst doing this.

The Journey Begins

The Journey Begins

Q: With skeptics and ridicule, all of this negativity and manufactured agro, risk, huge effort and exhaustion, why would anyone be bothered becoming a psychic reader?
A: Because people need the help that only a psychic can offer!

Though this is the final chapter in this book this is not the end. This is the beginning of your journey. You don't have to go through your journey alone, afraid and naked like I did. I am with you as Kushog, my Tibetan teacher remains with me. But that is the beginning of a story for another time.

In this book I have taught you how to do simple things properly. When mastered, these skills will help you to bring your life into harmony with everything. You no longer have to be life's victim, sabotaging yourself by hitting all the pot holes on the journey. You can master life. I know. I did!

As your life becomes more magical, things will go better for you, you will become stronger, more empowered, more capable and able to assist things to go better for others. Practising these seven skills will continue to strengthen you.

Though the practical skills are quickly acquired and easily remembered, there is a depth and breadth that can be added to your first steps. There are other psychic tools, the use of which will augment your readings, like:
- Tarot cards
- Tea and coffee cup readings

- Palmistry
- Runes
- Crystal ball work and scrying
- Pendulums, dowsing and divining
- Dreams interpretation etc.

The above will be set out for you in practical and easy steps in future publications.

See Your Way Clearly
I know that so far life has not gone the way that you wanted, but now you will be able to see your way clearly. Because you can see a little further down the road than most others, you will know how to avoid life's pot holes. People will begin to rely upon you for your guidance direction and strength because you are relying on yourself. You will become the clear, calm pool of reflection for them. You will become a master navigator on this journey called life. It is an adventure but for you it is no longer an adventure into the unknown.

I am proud of you.
Blessings on your journey.
Shé

Seven Psychic Secrets

A Final Word On Ethics and Equilibrium

Q: Why do people feel the need to have a psychic reading?
A: They need to know who they are.

Three millennia ago the psychic Delphic Oracle declared *"Know Thyself."* Healing, empowerment, clarity and direction are all by-products of the journey of personal exploration an individual embarks upon by engaging a psychic. This deceptive world teaches people to mistrust everything even themselves. Understanding your own psyche is a process of regaining deep self-trust and understanding for which the skilled psychic can be the guide.

The Divine Human Psyche

Psyche is the Goddess of the deep and true self or the soul. It is from her name that we derive words that describe this search, such as Psychic, Psychologist and Psychiatry. All of the practitioners of these arts seek to heal individual's deep inner wounds.

Lucius Apuleius, the author of "The Fable of Cupid and Psyche," born in Roman Africa about 125 A.D. was a lecturer in Platonic philosophy and a priest of Isis. The fable is based upon the philosophical doctrines of the classical mystery schools. This story fascinates those in the world of art, literature, philosophy, and psychiatry, and has been interpreted in various ways according to personal belief.

In the myth, Psyche is deceived by the world around her and doubts herself, resulting in her loosing everything she holds dear. The rest of the story is a symbolical search of the mortal soul for the true strength of it own nature.

Misunderstanding this journey through the human condition, many today become caught up in proving their own inner strength by engaging in the game of "See what horrors I have endured." A good reader frees the client from the foolish choices of this self-harm for self-worth cycle.

The Fool's Journey
'The Fool's Journey,' as outlined in the major arcana of the tarot, can be travelled from start to finish by a client in one successful reading. They can go from recklessly meandering through life and begin to cautiously seek what lies beneath, beyond and around the next bend. A good reader can facilitate an awakening in the client, beyond being caught up in mundane issues, that helps them realise that they have all of the elements surrounding them to create the things they most want in the world.

The answers to these questions that trouble the client cannot be found by looking anywhere outside, the answers they seek lay veiled within themselves. A psychic's job is to put the client back in touch with his or her own intuition. The skilled reader will get a client to listen to their own gut feelings, not their heart, nor their head. That feeling in the pit of the stomach chakra never lies.

Parts of the Soul

The chakra system can be described as an examination of parts of the human soul. By working with the chakras you can help heal various parts of your client's inner being that are affecting various parts of their life. Refer to the table in chapter two.

Positions of Trust

To be a reader is rewarding but it is a great responsibility. Vulnerable people seek a reader's help and place the reader in a position of trust. Always proceed with caution. Any abuse of this position of trust can wound the client emotionally and spiritually for life. Any one who abuses this position of trust should be reported to The Australian Psychic Association.[1]

Readers must also protect themselves. On a mundane level it is a good idea to obtain a blue card from your local police station to prove that you are safe to work with children and a yellow card to prove you are trusted to work with disabled people. The police checks required to obtain these accreditations are a protection for you as well as the client. These accreditations place you a step above reproach and show that you are willing to put in effort to prove your trustworthiness.

Emotional Dependence

It is tempting for a reader to become the client's crutch. A needy client can manoeuvre a reader into accepting too much responsibility for their problems by playing the victim or via guilt. Never allow your client to assume the "poor me" role. To do so would leave the reader open to being used or drained of energy and resources.

Always reinforce the fact that the client is totally in control of all of the choices in their life. As with parenting, sensitive but tough love is required to best facilitate your client's personal growth.

Equilibrium
If the reader is upset, or out of balance, they cannot become the clear, calm pool of reflection for their client. You cannot take your personal stuff into this working environment. If you can't leave it at the door then leave it alone. Your client will be far better off if you reschedule to a time when you can regain your equilibrium.

Check Your Ego At The Door
If a person becomes a reader because they want to be known as a great guru or saviour then they defiantly are going to do more damage than good. Being a professional psychic is not about being right, and it is not about how many cool, weird, tricks you can do. Being a psychic reader is about being of service. You do it because you feel compelled to help. Nor can you build up a sense of self-worth by playing at being less than everyone else. An inverted ego does not work for psychics. You just have to be what you are.

You cannot play the poverty stricken martyr. Practising for free means that your client ends up owing you a karmic debit and that just gets messy. Like any other specialist service you deserve fair remuneration for your services. No one expects any specialist to work for free and you are a specialist that has put years into study and training. Debits must be paid and spiritual debits even more so.

Rewards

Having said all of this, I can tell you from personal experience that there is nothing more rewarding than working as a professional psychic. Watching people open up and flower in front of you, helping them find answers, gain peace and closure, seeing them finally understand and break negative patterns than have plagued then through lifetimes, receiving the letters of thanks and appreciation from them and their children and even saving lives, are the things that make this job so worthwhile.

Though the world is far from being saved and this work is tough and tiring, when you lay your head on your pillow at night, your rest will be deep and untroubled because you know that... "Today, I made a difference for that person."

Shé Speaks to Packed Houses Around The World

Shé has run Psychic development courses for the last 25 years for approximately 60,000 people here and overseas. Many well know psychics have had their skills honed by her. Shé has educated far more by writing for dozens of alternative magazines in Australia and overseas, and by her public speaking appearances at large festivals such as The Body, Mind and Spirit, Nexus Conferences, Aquarius Festival, The International Gathering of Shaman, Conscious Living, The Goddess Conference and T other Australian psychic expos to name just a few. Shé incorporates Psychic training for the beginner and the advanced practitioner into her hectic touring schedule. To take advantage of her coerces on The Craft, The Tarot, Tantra, Mediumship, Magick, Health, Financial Embetterment Security, Indigenous Cultures, Working with the Earth , The Universe and Psychic Development etc. when she comes to a town near you see: -

www.shambhallah.org

Wanda Shipton

Our cover artist is the amazing Wanda Shipton (B.A. Psychology) is an internationally acclaimed visionary artist who has channelled tens of thousands of pictures for people of their spirit guides. More startling is the fact that the image is totally unique for each individual. Wand is a skilled reader in her own right with 30-years experience. This isn't highly surprising as she is a direct descendant of the famous 18th centaury English prophetess mother Shipton. Wanda is also further tied into the family by marriage.

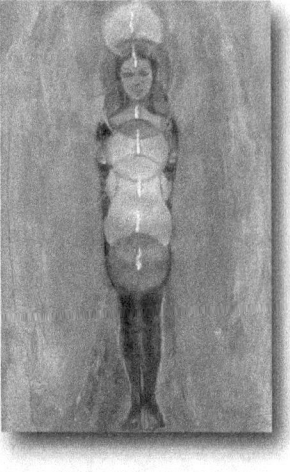

Wanda Shipton was born in post-war Britain to parents who never quite understood why their little girl was different. "Even as a very small child I would have visions of the spirit world. In fact, they were more than visions, I often felt a part of the spirit world. Of course I didn't understand it then, but somehow it didn't seem particularly strange to me," said Wanda, who now calls the Gold Coast home. "I would experience the presence of spirits in the form of colours and shapes, and very often sounds too. What's more even as a small girl I would often have out-of-body experiences. I often tried explaining to my parents and relatives what was happening to me, but they would invariably put it down to the ramblings of a child with an overactive imagination," she said.

Spirit Guides

During a session Wanda tunes in to the person to visualise their spirit guide, and then proceeds to channel messages. At the same time she draws an image of the guide. The guides offer direction in life, as well as enhancing your sense of fulfilment and wellbeing. "Once the guide starts talking through me to the person in front of me any scepticism or doubt that may have previously existed instantly dissipates," Wanda said. "The guides have information about that person that only they could know. I am merely a channel. It is the guides who are speaking – not me." Contact Wanda on wandashipton@yahoo.com or see more of her work on her website

White Eagle Woman
by Wanda Shipton

www.wandashipton.com

Seven Psychic Secrets

List of Images and Image Credits

Page	Description	Credit
Cover	Angelic Chakra Fire	© Wanda Shipton 2009 with kind permission
Background chapter heading image	The Happy Medium Logo	Egyptian hieroglyphic symbol for the Goddess Heka, the Goddess of science and magick. Also the source of the later Greek Goddess Hekaté © Shé D'Montford 1996
Page 9	Houdini and Margery the Medium with members of Scientific American	Houdini Images Wakimedia Commons
Page 10 top	Front page of Boston Newspaper 1924	Houdini Images Wikimedia Commons
Page 10 bottom	Front Page Houdini's Pamphlet defaming Margery the Boston Medium	Houdini Images Wikimedia Commons
Page 11	Front cover "The Secret Life of Houdini" The Making of America's First Superhero (Hardcover)	Atria; 1st Atria Books edition (October 31, 2006)
Page 13	Houdini Photo postcard signed "My Two Sweethearts" Houdini with his mother and wife, 1907."	Houdini Images Wikimedia Commons
Page 14	Arthur Ford	Royalty Free Image 1929
Page 15	Facsimile of Statement by Bess Houdini	Royalty free image as see on www.useyourmagic.com/essays/houdini.html Essay by Tom Razzeto and www.survivalafterdeath.org.uk/.../houdini.htm Article by Arthur Ford -
Page 26	Synthetic zincite crystals	Author graphic from royalty free images
Page 29	Vitruvian circuit	Author graphic from royalty free images
Page 30	Mind reading machine	Reproduced with the kind permission of Emotive Systems Australia 2009
Page 31	Images read from the mind of a cat	Royalty free with credit to Garrett Stanley compliments of Wiki Media Images
Page 47	Table – Amazing 108	Well known equations and facts about the number 108
Page 50	Table – Bhuh Bhuvah Svah	Table of correspondences by author © Shé D'Montford 1996
Page 64	Simulated aura image of the author	Photo - Marie Rudd 1996

Page 65 & Page 66	Actual aura photography of author	1989 & 1995
Page 73	The Chakras	Johann George Gichtel 1874
Page 74	Chakra Table	© Shé D'Montford 1996
Page 99	The author picking up Ken Wills	Ray Hobby 2004
Page 108	The author with Alison Dubois and Thomas Owen at the Mind, Body and Spirit Festival. Sydney. Australia.	Ken Wills 2007
Page 110	The author performing the wedding of Susan and Shannon Lacy	With permission from the couple 2002
Page 116	Classical ouroboros Image	Classical ouroboros Image royalty free
Page 122	Earth/Water/Fire Air Mudras	Ken Wills 2010
Page 127	The author speaking in Toowoomba	Jenny Gersekowski 2008
Page 138	Freddie Mercury, The King, With a Sweatband	Royalty free image compliments of The Aussie Queens Fan Club
Page 140	Shé with Skip Atwater former head of the U.S. Military Psychic Spying Unit	The author 2001
Page 170	Spinal Chart	Royalty Free Image
Page 181	The author speaking to a Sold-Out, standing room only crowd in Toowoomba	Ken Wills 2008

Index

Page 24	Ancient Mysteries = Modern Science
Page 112	Angels
Page 16	Answering The Modern Skeptic
Page 172	Arrhythmia and Tachycardia
Page 173	Asthma
Page 39	Be Calm and Clear
Page 89	Bioelectric And Radio Frequency Generation
Page 172	Bowl Movements
Page 40	Breath Connects Us All
Page 109	Calling In Spirit
Page 119	Calling In The "The Watchers" To Guard Over You
Page 121	Calling In The Elemental Guardians
Page 72	Chakras
Page 152	Changing Fate
Page 48	Chanting
Page 181	Check Your Ego At The Door
Page 172	Childhood Behavioural Problems
Page 102	Children Need Prana Donors
Page 61	Children See Things
Page 117	Clairvoyance Game
Page 152	Client Confidentiality and Psychic Ethics
Page 2	Contents
Page 97	Cooling Down Game
Page 27	Crystals
Page 21	Dark Side
Page 3	Dedication
Page 134	Delayed Verification
Page 68	Dharana
Page 171	Digestive Problems
Page 87	Disaster Avoidance Consciousness
Page 124	Dismissing The Elements
Page 178	Divine Human Psyche

Page 68	Dominant Eye
Page 122	East
Page 124	East
Page 90	Electricity, Nerves and Chakras
Page 120	Elemental Attributions
Page 180	Emotional Dependence
Page 81	Energy Bubble Game
Page 173	Epilepsy and Motion Sickness
Page 181	Equilibrium
Page 113	Fay Realm
Page 78	Feeling, Moving and Directing Energy
Page 178	Final Word On Ethics and Equilibrium
Page 179	Fool's Journey
Page 190	Foot Notes
Page 46	Gâyatrî Mantra
Page 113	Guides
Page 62	Hands of Light Game
Page 13	Harry Comes Back
Page 8	Harry Houdini - A Paranormal Believer and Skeptic
Page 173	Head Cold Congestion
Page 171	Headache
Page 159	Healing and Remote Healing
Page 165	Healing and Remote Healing Game
Page 94	Heating Up Game
Page 51	Hidden Mathematical Context
Page 36	How it Works
Page 58	How to See Auras
Page 91	Human Battery Potentials
Page 26	Human Crystal Radio Sets
Page 89	Human Electricity
Page 187	Index
Page 44	Inspiration
Page 43	Inspiration Is Breathing In
Page 155	Intimacy and Tact

Seven Psychic Secrets

Page 176	Journey Begins
Page 67	Know Thy Self
Page 106	Learning to Work With Spirit
Page 55	Lessons For Psychic Skills
Page 98	Lifting Game - Levitation Exercises
Page 185	List of Images and Image Credits
Page 59	Living In A Larger World
Page 154	Living With Nobility, Freedom and Responsibility
Page 23	Looking At The Past To See The Future
Page 45	Mantra
Page 49	Meaning of the Gâyatrî
Page 150	Medical Intuition
Page 156	Medical Intuition Game
Page 171	Memory Loss
Page 25	Methods Preserved In The Mystery
Page 30	Mind Reading Machines
Page 69	Mirror Game
Page 32	My Task As A Teacher
Page 51	My Translation of The Gâyatrî
Page 151	Non-Competitiveness
Page 122	North
Page 125	North
Page 62	Nothing Is Lost Forever
Page 16	One Last Theatrical Message
Page 111	Opening the Crown Chakra
Page 131	Opening The Heart Chakra
Page 52	Other Mantras For You To Try
Page 119	Others
Page 180	Parts of the Soul
Page 153	Plato's warning - The Moral of Atlantis
Page 180	Positions of Trust
Page 47	Power Up Game
Page 126	Practical Application of Psychic Abilities
Page 39	Prana

Page 19	Psychic Science
Page 28	Psychic Technologies
Page 101	Psychic Vampires
Page 53	Psychic Work Room
Page 130	Psychometry
Page 132	Psychometry Game
Page 24	Quantum Mechanics
Page 58	Remembering
Page 166	Remote Healing
Page 142	Remote Viewing
Page 145	Remote Viewing and Ethics
Page 146	Remote Viewing Game
Page 143	Remote Viewing Is The Most Lucrative Psychic Skill
Page 182	Rewards
Page 70	Samadhi Pants
Page 18	Science Knows 96% Of Nothing
Page 177	See Your Way Clearly
Page 138	Seeing Freddy From My Side
Page 46	Sing It To Remember It
Page 11	Skeptical Hysteria
Page 166	Soul Retrieval
Page 123	South
Page 125	South
Page 114	Spirits of Dead
Page 113	Spirits of Nature
Page 115	Spirits of Planets
Page 116	Spirits of Time
Page 163	Taking the Faith Out of Healing
Page 118	Talking To The Animals Game
Page 52	The Charm
Page 17	The One
Page 42	Theta State
Page 117	Totem Spirits
Page 171	Traditional Spiritual Healing Methods

Page 92	Tumo As Body Heating
Page 92	Tumo Masters In Tibet
Page 109	Two Main Rules Of Working With Spirit
Page 111	Types of Spirits
Page 84	Unbending Arm
Page 103	Using Prana with Conscious Intent
Page 184	Wanda Shipton
Page 93	Warming
Page 123	West
Page 125	West
Page 100	What Is This Power And Strength?
Page 33	What You Will Learn
Page 100	Where Does This Power Come From?
Page 47	Why 108 Times?
Page 5	Why It Works
Page 17	Why It Works
Page 6	Why? It Works!
Page 6	Word To The Skeptics
Page 107	You Can Learn To Communicate With Spirit
Page 65	Your Own Spirit or Ghost
Page 40	Zigi -Ten Breath Meditation

FOOT NOTES

Chapter 1

1)
Although it is commonly accepted that the basic concepts of 'Health Promotion' have been developed in the last two decades, they have their roots in ancient civilizations and in particular in Greek antiquity. As evident from medical and philosophical documents of the sixth to fourth centuries B.C. Notably Pythagorean philosophy.
http://heapro.oxfordjournals.org/cgi/content/abstract/24/2/185

The abandonment of hygiene as an old-fashioned, pagan superstition was welcomed by the Church, owing to her horror of sex and nudity, and was fostered by her with dire consequences for mankind. Not only were the classic Greek and Roman images and statues of nudes destroyed, clad or painted over in most of Europe, but the public thermae that had done so much to keep the ancient Greek and Roman people healthy, were closed down. Body washing and even just looking at one's own nudity were considered evidence of sinfulness and depravity, and the few people who were sometimes ordered by their physician to take a bath were lowered into the tub fully clothed. To this day, for the rare baths in some Italian parochial boarding schools, a chaste bathing suit must be worn in the tub, and mirrors are absent.
All the medical historians (Sigerist, Dubos, Inglis) concur that the disappearance of the great medieval epidemics, including the bubonic plague which wiped out nearly half of Europe, was not due to the introduction of any specific therapy, but to the introduction of hygiene, of the sewer system and clean water in the cities, and that the startling improvements these institutions brought, raising life expectancy dramatically, started half a century before large-scale vaccination was adopted. Oddly enough, it did not seem to occur to any of those historians that what they defined as the "mysterious" insurgence of those epidemics, was not mysterious at all but the inevitable consequence of Church-supported Galenism, i.e. the abandonment of Hippocratic hygiene. The disastrous plagues of the Middle Ages were the legitimate offspring of the sad, long-lasting union between the sexual phobia of the Church and the extrapolation to man of observations made on animals, which, for instance, don't need washing with lots of soap and hot water after bringing forth, because the antiseptic effect of their own saliva is sufficient to prevent puerperal fever. Today, pestilences keep turning up wherever populations are crowded and cleanliness is absent. In unhygienic southern Italy, puerperal fever causes as many deaths as a century ago.
http://www.animalvoices.org/ADAV/page5.htm

..In 1800 The level of hygiene was very poor. Surgeons operated in dirty theatres and used instruments that were rarely washed between operations. They did not wash their hands before or between operations, or wear clean clothes.
http://encyclopedia.farlex.com/medicine.+19th-century

1546 -- Italian physician Girolamo Fracastoro outlines theory of contagious disease. He reasoned that infectious diseases could be passed on in 3 ways: simple contact, indirect contact (e.g., bedclothes) and minute bodies over distance through the air. Thus, isolation and disinfection were the ways to take action against epidemics. http://es.rice.edu/ES/humsoc/Galileo/Catalog/Files/fracstro.html
https://php.radford.edu/~wkovarik/drupal/?q=node/15

2)
Bruce Cathie
In Nexus Magazine, OCT/NOV 1994 Issue. - PO box 177, Kempton, IL 60946-0177

Seven Psychic Secrets

815-253-6464

3)
Melbourne Sun Herald, Saturday, February 4, 2006
'THE DARKNESS INSIDE OF EVERYTHING' by Katherine Kizilos, page 17 of the Features in the Melbourne Sun Herald. Saturday, February 4, 2006

4)
Regardless of how the classify themselves many argue that that being a skeptic means "embracing a belief system of not believing in things" the motivator being to feel superior to other belief systems which is central to any dogma.
http://www.adherents.com/
Retired Lawyer of the Supreme Court of New South Wales, and the High Court of Australia, Victor Zammit in his article A LAWYER ON THE SKEPTICS
  claims that FUNDING CLOSED-MINDED SKEPTICS IS LIKE POURING MONEY DOWN THE DRAIN - Closed-minded skeptics don't get results
http://www.victorzammit.com/skeptics/fundingskeptics.html
The Inquiring Neutral Skeptic website admits that "skepticism means to suspend judgement" yet this rarely happens.
Skeptic John Jackson in his article on What is Skepticism? -An overview of what skepticism actually is.. has to admit that skeptics "often have opinions that are at odds with many people's beliefs"
Beginning with an opinion is a belief!

Chapter 2
1)
Making Your Own Japa-mala
You will need 107 beads about the size of a pea and 1 larger.
Thread the 107 beads loosely on to a string then thread on your larger bead.
Tie off the string near the larger bead leaving about 1/2 a cm of slack so that the beads may be moved easily by your fingers whilst performing recitations.
With your eyes closed, slide each of the beads along the string, one for each recitations of a mantra. When you get back to the larger bead you will know that you have completed 108 recitations.

2)
"http://www.wildideas.net/cathbad/pagan/dr-guide2.html"

Chapter 3
1)
http://www.thefreelibrary.com/Electrifying+biology%3B+biological+systems+naturally+produce+...-a03743626.

Chapter 4
1)
Deosil (Wiccan spelling) or deiseal (scottish gaelic) likewise means "with the sun", i.e. anti-clockwise in southern hemisphere!
Sunwise is different in the two hemispheres!

Chapter 5
1) See the Daily Telegraph story via the link below...
http://www.dailytelegraph.com.au/news/is-this-ned-kellys-skull/story-e6freuy9-122579711068

Chapter 8
1)For more details about this research and results details see "No Faith Required" _© 1995 Eikstine Publications. Norway ISBN 82-90601-09-3

Chapter 10
1) **LIST OF PSYCHIC ASSOCIATIONS**

The Ethical Society of Psychics ESP
http://www.esp.org.au
Australian Psychic Association
psicomgroup@msn.com.au
http://newagesupastore.com/apa/apa.php
United Kingdom Association of Psychics
http://www.ukassociationofpsychics.co.uk/
American Association of Psychics
http://www.americanassociationofpsychics.com/
Canadian Psychic Association
http://www.canadianassociationofpsychics.com/

International Spiritualist Organisations
http://www.harmonygrovespiritualist.org/
http://www.theisf.com/
http://en.wikipedia.org/wiki/List_of_Spiritualist_organizations
http://www.isacanada.ca/

Other Useful Psychic Association and Research Centre Links
International Remote Viewing Association
http://www.irva.org/
Koestler Parapsychology Lab
http://moebius.psy.ed.ac.uk/
Parapsychological Association
http://www.parapsych.org/
Princeton Engineering Anomalies Research
http://www.princeton.edu/~pear/
PRV Associates
http://www.prvassociates.com/
Psi Explorer
http://www.psiexplorer.com/
Scottish Society for Psychic Research
http://www.sspr.co.uk/
Society for Psychical Research
http://www.spr.ac.uk/
Universal Psychic Guild
http://www.psychicguild.com/
American Tarot Association
http://www.ata-tarot.com/index.htm
Canadian Tarot Network
http://www.tarotcanada.com/index.html
Tarot Guild of Australia
http://www.tarotguild.org.au/
Australian Academy of Hypnosis
http://www.mindmotivations.com/
Australian Spiritual Churches
http://www.geocities.com/actspiritualists/churches.htm

Seven Psychic Secrets

www.ingramcontent.com/pod-product-compliance
Lightning Source LLC
Chambersburg PA
CBHW071919290426
44110CB00013B/1413